WAITING FOR RAIN

/////////////////////////////////////

WAITING FOR RAIN

A Farmer's Story

DAN BUTTERWORTH

ALGONQUIN BOOKS
OF CHAPEL HILL

Published by
ALGONQUIN BOOKS OF CHAPEL HILL
Post Office Box 2225
Chapel Hill, North Carolina 27515-2225

a division of
WORKMAN PUBLISHING COMPANY, INC.
708 Broadway
New York, New York 10003

Excerpt from "Gerontion" in *Collected Poems 1909–1962* by T. S. Eliot, copyright 1936 by Harcourt, Brace, Jovanovich, Inc. and Faber and Faber Ltd., copyright © 1964, 1963 by T.S. Eliot, reprinted by permission of the publishers.

LIBRARY OF CONGRESS CATALOGING-IN-PUBLICATION DATA
Butterworth, Dan, 1955–
    Waiting for rain : a farmer's story / Dan Butterworth.
      p.   cm.
    ISBN 0-945575-78-5
    1. Farm life—North Carolina. 2. Farmers—North Carolina.
    3. Agriculture—Economic aspects—North Carolina. I.
Title.   91-28611
    S521.5.N8B87 1992   CIP
    630'.9756—dc20

10 9 8 7 6 5 4 3 2 1

FIRST PRINTING

for Charlie

Here I am, an old man in a dry month,

Being read to by a boy, waiting for rain.

T. S. Eliot

CONTENTS

ACKNOWLEDGMENTS

I would like to thank Archie, Waynette, Alec, Anne, and Cathy Clare for their invaluable time, candor, and generosity, without which the writing of this book would have been impossible. I also want to thank the late Dick Brown, whose newspaper articles, written decades ago, gave me a glimpse of past life on the inner coastal plain and Sandhills of North Carolina. Finally, many thanks to Louis Rubin for his interest in the manuscript, to Shannon Ravenel for patient and excellent editing, to Amy Ryan for her copyediting, to the North Carolina Collection at The University of North Carolina at Chapel Hill, to Sally Tonkin, and to my wife, Beth Cooley.

A NOTE ON NAMES

While the people, places, and events described in the following pages are real, location and personal names have been changed for the sake of privacy.

WAITING FOR RAIN

////////////////

PROLOGUE

IN THE YEAR of the drought, Archie Clare was sixty years old and stood six feet above the soil. He had an intelligent, thoughtful face. His black hair was silvering at his temples, and though it had receded a bit, it grew thick and wiry around his head. His prominent and perfectly straight nose jutted out between deep-set eyes of cold cobalt blue. Sharp vertical lines had formed from his chin to the middle of his cheeks, and around his eyes were the wrinkles of a face that regularly folded itself into a squint. The jutting brow and nose gave him something of the look of both bird and badger.

During that summer of 1986, between terms at the university, I taught part-time at a small college near a town I will call Farlanboro, the county seat of Lothian County. Located on the southern reaches of the North Carolina Sandhills and the western margin of the inner coastal plain, one hundred miles west of the Atlantic and fifteen miles north of South Carolina, Farlanboro is a small town with a population of eleven thousand and a downtown business district occupying roughly six blocks. No building is over four stories tall. Two heavily used railroad tracks running north to south define the western border of downtown. Like many small towns in North Carolina, Farlanboro has lost much of the little vitality its business district ever had to malls that have sprung up where fields of cotton and corn grew just seasons ago. In Wayfare, the tiny town where Archie grew up, ten miles north of Farlanboro, the farms can still be seen from Main Street.

By chance, Archie and Waynette Clare, parents of friends, said that they had a room for me in their four-bedroom home on the edge of town. They had raised three children, two girls and a boy, who had left their hometown to live elsewhere. One daughter taught college in Virginia, the other worked in an art museum in Washington, D.C. The son was a carpenter in Raleigh. Waynette Clare taught French in the county high school and often spent a part of the summer leading European tours for people from her community. Archie Clare farmed for a living. He grew to-bacco, corn, soybeans, wheat, and some produce—canta-loupes, watermelons, cucumbers—depending on demand, his interest, and the weather. Archie normally farmed two plots of Waynette's family's land, one about eleven miles south near the South Carolina border and the other about fifteen miles southeast in Campbell County. Sometimes he would lease additional acreage near one of those two farms.

The summer of 1986 was so hot and dry that Archie spent a lot of time at home. Since I only taught one or two classes in the mornings and had the afternoons and week-ends to myself, we began to sit together in the yard early in the morning and to linger over coffee and iced tea on the back porch after lunch. It was only natural that our conver-sation turned to farming. If Archie had lived on the land he farmed he probably would have found some way to work with the crops even as they failed, or he would simply have watched them suffer the way an anxious young parent watches a feverish newborn sleep. But since he ate and slept in the air-conditioning of his home in Farlanboro, perhaps it was an obscure guilt that compelled him to make the farms and the crops the sole subject of his conversations. If the only thing left to do was to plow and fertilize and irri-gate with language, then that's what he would do. Archie seemed to think that words have a way of keeping some things alive. His stories about seasons saved from disaster by later windfall rains and stories about seasons of complete failure from which he had recovered both nurtured his hopes for redemption from the current drought and distracted him from the unlikelihood of such a turnaround. When he discovered that I was interested in the details of his farming, he began to take me down to the fields with him to show me around. As the drought settled in and gave him less to do, our conversations focused more and more on what he called the predicament of the farmer. And we would drive in the heat and look at the crop and talk about the good seasons and the bad.

/ / / / /

Archie's situation posed unique impediments to the success of his business. He lived at a distance from the land that he farmed; he didn't own that land and so had to distribute whatever profits he garnered; he needed to keep a tenant family at the Sinclair farm in order to watch the equipment; and he incurred the extra expense of transportation. But these elements also turned him into a reflective man who had the time and inclination to make sense of his predicament. Before the muscle work of the day began he would have the meditative drive to the farm. And between various operations he would have to climb into his truck, his tractor, or his combine and drive some more. All that driving gave him time to think and, when I accompanied him, to talk. Maybe that is why his views struck me as so valuable. He had an objectivity that allowed him to watch and assess his actions even as he performed them.

Archie could ponder his circuit as a constellation of sites or as a series of events in time. When most people think of the cycles of the farming year they think of the rising and falling of crops the way they might appear in a cartoon flip book. According to Archie's experience, there's something to the cartoon view. But Archie knew just how complicated the business of growing a crop could be. Come January he'd have thirty-five to fifty acres in winter wheat. In late March he'd apply a topdressing of nitrogen to those acres with the tractor and that'd be all he'd have to do on wheat until harvest. The land he planned to put into tobacco and corn during the spring he would in late winter turn to a depth of a foot or less with a chisel or moldboard plow, mounted behind the tractor. On a small section of land near the field where he would grow his tobacco crop, Archie would bed the tobacco seeds in long strips covered with plastic. Usually he would plant the seeds sometime in February, and after about ten weeks or so he would transplant the seedlings into the field.

In March Archie would start leveling the fields for his summer crops, fields that he had already chiseled or plowed with a disk. Usually he would broadcast fertilizer just before disking. Corn would go in at the last of March or first of April. Tobacco would be transplanted from the beds between April 15 and the tenth of May. By the time he was planting tobacco, the corn would be up. During the few years Archie grew cotton he would plant it between mid-April and May 1. His soybeans would be in by May 15.

Soy, corn, and cotton are all seed crops. Easy planting. But planting tobacco takes helpers, two per row, who sit on the planter attached to the tractor. They have to drop the plants one by one, spaced anywhere from twenty-two to thirty inches apart, depending on the farmer's style and aims. Planted farther apart, the plants grow bigger leaves, producing the same poundage but requiring less handwork during picking. If the farmer uses an herbicide, which most do, he applies it early. A preemerge herbicide goes on before disking, and a postemerge herbicide goes on after the seeds are in the ground. All that costs like hell, requires careful timing, and depends on the cooperation of the elements. Plant one day, postemerge herbicide the next day, and then rain the next, ideally.

Archie thinks of farming in the days of his father as entailing a very different set of activities from those he must perform today. This is as much due to the preponderance of paper in his life as it is to the distance between the tracts he farms. The old cycle of plow, plant, grow, and harvest revolves now within the shadow of the new overarching cycle embodied in serpentine legal phrases of loan statements that govern the farmer by dividing his life and years into semiannual seasons: a time to borrow, a time to repay.

The efficiency of any process that exchanges energy for a product naturally comes under question, for energy—in the farmer's case the various fuels of funds, food, and gasoline—is easily wasted. And though energy may be lost in many ways, none more closely resembles the weevil in the corn than interest on debt. In an imperfect world people will always find means to profit from others' losses, so Archie thinks. Thus the inefficiencies of the paper cycle feather the bankers' nests.

This larger cycle of borrow and repay remains abstract as long as its transactions represent wealth through checks, credit statements, and various other papers. And the larger cycle of paper wealth has become almost completely divorced from the seasons of spring, summer, fall, and winter. Crop reduction program payments may not show up in the mailbox for more than eighteen months after a harvest. Tax and loan repayment schedules can make every month as cruel as winter. Who can predict when Archie will need to go to the bank for a loan reassessment? It is precisely this abstractness of the farming business that leads farmers to overextend themselves or to find bad news at the same time a bumper crop is being harvested.

Regardless of how just or unjust the system is, regardless of how well or poorly Archie understands the economics of the farming system, year after year he has to participate in it in order to get the money to carry on, to gas up his truck, to put food on the table. The papers on his desk remain a poor translation of the sweat and thought that go into Archie's daily work, and every time he sits down to the documents it is with a sense of their unreality. Each day Archie travels a circuit that grounds the various abstractions of bank notices, account summaries, crop certificates, and theories of value in the realities of sandy soil, parched crops, and piney woods, in a world that alternately yields the satisfactions of useful labor and the frustrations of fuzzy conversation, healthy wheat and exhausted fields.

The circumstances of Archie Clare's farm business were established long ago, and at times he can view his situation with the objectivity of a crow over an empty field. But Archie Clare is no nearer a sound retirement now than when he left the air force thirty years ago. A bank account containing the money Archie cleared during all the years he worked the farms would contain nothing. Yes, he earned enough each year to clothe and feed and raise his children, and there was always enough, along with Waynette's income, to make a life for the family. But money remains just another seasonal phenomenon in Archie Clare's life. What he has borrowed in order to spin his wheels for a time he has always paid back, and then some. Whenever he had big profits in the good years, he had to pay off large debts or reinvest in machinery, in labor, in the next season's crop.

It was only recently that Archie caught on, so he says, to the illusion of prosperity that all the paper creates. On paper he has had a good year, but he now knows that the subsidy he earned on tobacco might not show up in his checkbook for two years, and when it does come it is likely to be far less than what he's expecting. Now he knows why the bank considers him a sound investment even when he's failed to realize a profit the year before. Now he knows what it means to look at the house, the cars, the truck, the machinery, and the land—the things that go into making up a life—as assets. It means to imagine what it would be like to make a life without them.

/ / / / /

When I first met Archie Clare I was intrigued by the contradictions of his manner. It was mid-June, but June had come with a burly heat that usually didn't hit until well into July. The temperature had broken one hundred several times, and drought had all but arrested Archie's activity. There was no nervousness in his gestures and actions, yet his words revealed that he was so disillusioned with the farming system that he contemplated quitting. He had always been known as a quiet man, and he usually was. But those who knew him well knew he could talk avidly for hours about subjects that interested him. When engaged by conversation he could be polite to a fault, but when faced by company that bored him, he would tolerate the chat for a few moments, then simply excuse himself and go off to take a nap.

If it is possible to define a person according to a simple gesture or movement, his would be the fishing for a cigarette. His hands, like those of anyone whose tenure on existence is secured solely by what his hands grasp, were reminiscent of roots freshly pulled out of soil. Rough, dark, flecked, with variegated cracks and scales. The elegant counterpositioning of thumb and forefinger no longer seemed as amazing as the sheer ability of these misused, swollen fingers to move at all. He would tap his shirt pocket, locate the package he sought, and with a delicacy and singularity of purpose and motion extract his smoke. It seemed miraculous that these fingers could select a cigarette out of its package, could tap end on end and raise it to the mouth and scrape a tiny wheel over flint.

There was something else about Archie Clare's life and manner that struck me as remarkable, and it had to do with the fact that he lived in isolation. He did not participate in any of the activities that connect people in a public life. Archie's society consisted of Waynette and the handful of people he associated with through his work. Farlanboro did not have a single tavern where he might have gone to talk with other farmers. Archie no longer went to church, he avoided the community softball games, and he never participated in fraternal and civic organizations. The land he worked and the trees that shaded him provided his only immediate company.

/////

Farlanboro lies toward the southern end of Lothian County where the land is so flat that standing in an open field will convince anyone that the universe is composed entirely of sky and that the most singular feature of the earth is distance. Part of the inner coastal plain, southern Lothian and Campbell counties, where Archie lives and farms, are broken up by stretches of loblolly pine and intermittent swamps. According to topographical maps, Lothian and Campbell counties have largely been stripped of their forests, but from the ground there appear to be plenty of trees. On low, wet ground grow sweet gum, black gum, cypress, tulip poplar, beech, red maple, white and red oak, willow oak, sassafras, and hickory. On the higher ground pines abound where the soil is composed of marginally fertile ivory sand, which is also excellent for the production of tobacco.

Covering the northern portion of Lothian County are the longleaf pines and scrub-oak forests of the Sandhills, which form a wedge between the Piedmont and the inner coastal plain. The Sandhills were formed millions of years ago by a recession of the sea so rapid that it left the inland dunes behind; the sands of the inner coastal plain were deposited by a more leisurely retreat. Turkey oak, bluejack oak, and post oak saplings seem starved underneath the longleaf pines. Wax myrtle, sweet bay, and dwarf huckleberry grow where frequent fires have promoted pine over hardwoods. Roads through the Sandhills rise and fall on crests and troughs that form perfect sine waves.

Physical description and geographical data cannot convey the singular remoteness of the part of the country Archie Clare calls home. I cannot help but locate the source of Archie's isolation in the nature of the land itself. The Sandhills and the bleak plains of Lothian and Campbell counties have always been unfathomable, if not nearly impenetrable, and this has kept it unknown territory. Setting off in any given precinct of the Sandhill forest offers the prospect of never coming back alive, of never finding yourself once you're lost, of heading in a straight line and not reaching civilization until starvation and dehydration have worked their will. The sparseness of the population contributes to the sense of wildness in the silence of the woods; the reticence of the inhabitants makes the present lack of public life in Farlanboro and Wayfare seem indigenous. In the early records of the region's explorers and settlers, writers often noted the desolation and uninhabitable wildness of the inland sands of Carolina. A review of the Lothian County records reinforces the impression that Archie Clare lives on the margin of history and culture. Since Lothian County was created early in the nineteen-hundreds from portions of two larger counties, it now stands on the periphery of more populous regions with documented histories.

Those county histories neglect the towns and the people who now are situated beyond the borders of their concerns. As a result, there isn't any real historical account of Lothian County to be found in libraries or historical collections.

The inaccessibility of the region is in its way a corollary to the absence of public life beyond high school in Lothian County. Farlanboro, the county seat, has its churches, its community softball, and its opportunities for the casual conversations that link fellow workers. But Farlanboro has no town square. There are no taverns, no halls in which dances are regularly held. Occasional meetings in grocery or hardware stores are not enough to break down the isolation of a person who works alone, not enough to reassure the solitary farmer that his successes and failures matter to anyone but himself. So, Archie Clare had his farming and his driving, an oblique connection with Waynette's society, and his irregular and enthusiastic meetings with strangers who could tell him news of the world. Archie's world pushed him inward, just as economy and history had driven his ancestors toward the interior of a remote land. Of course the blank spot on the map was home to him. I came to see that just as he inhabited a place scarcely known to the outside world, the places, voices, and faces of that region and past inhabited Archie's thoughts and thus populated the empty wilderness he drove through. The languor of summer and the flatness of time presented a world to him that I would never know. Driving in the truck with Archie Clare, I heard, the way a wakeful child hears grownups talking in another room, a tiny bit of his conversation with the people and land held in his memory.

When Archie drove he was insulated from the world by the bubble of his truck cab. When he worked he was usually alone. If he wasn't working alone he was isolated by the force of his concentration. And even when Archie was engaged in conversation he often maintained a withdrawn reserve as if he were talking aloud to himself. He made friends easily but seldom kept them, for he befriended people on the move or people as remote from the patterns of regular discourse as he was. Archie seemed to distrust the permanence or significance of human relations, and yet when he talked about people who were dead or far away it was with a familiarity and intimacy that revealed the extent to which they had occupied his thoughts.

The contradictions of Archie's life—his love and his hate for farming; the apathy that characterized his dealings with the living and the energy that characterized his dealings with the dead; his activity in a land and season that had the power to smother thought with their very immensity; the paradox of paper prosperity and failed cash flow—these revealed that Archie was living on the cusp of a very uncertain future. His actions tended to balance elegance and self-destruction in such a way that he made life seem little more than a pretty way of dying. When his fingers fumbled inside a transmission, gears, plates, clutch springs, and screws became extensions of him; his hands became dendrites and grease the medium through which messages scurried across the gaps that separated him from the world of dead weight and intolerable inertness. When he searched for lost keys or misplaced glasses, he'd tap at the pockets of his shirt like a doctor or explore the interior of his coat with the steady deliberateness of someone searching through a wallet he'd found for the owner's identification. Desk, mantelpiece, nightstand, and, finally, the kitchen countertop would receive his attention. And then, after spilling the keys into his pocket, he would tip back his hat, put a cigarette in his mouth, and walk out the back door. And these actions may tell all that Archie or anyone could know of what the future held for Archie Clare.

His patience and deliberateness in the face of drought and failure of the farm appeared as contradictions to me because, until I knew Archie Clare, I did not understand how life is lived in places beyond the reference of newspaper headlines, in places that occupy the spaces between the names on the map. I did not understand the paradoxes of life on the inner coastal plain of North Carolina, where farmers would rather have drought than too much rain, where farmers persist in a livelihood even after it proves inadequate to their needs, where farmers who have quit farming continue to farm.

The following observations were born in the cab of Archie's El Camino and move toward an imperfect understanding of the life of one farmer. This book traces the thoughts and movements of Archie Clare during the last days of his farming career and amounts to a vicarious farewell to one way of life in the United States. This is a story about living a particular life in a particular place in our time, an attempt to capture the look of an eye, the idiom of a face, the conversation of the elements, and the music of little words before they change so much that we forget what they were.

ONE

Long before the drought of 1986, Archie's experience growing up had taught him about the frailty of the farmer's enterprise, about the limited returns for the investment of time, about the way the land and the crop can take a lot from a human hand and give nothing back. But when he went into the business for himself, farming was still farming—a matter of putting seeds in the ground, helping them grow, harvesting the produce, and selling the goods. That's the way it always had been where he grew up.

Archie's story began where he was born, in Wayfare, a small town near the Lumber River in the southern region of the North Carolina Sandhills, ten miles north of Farlanboro. Archie was the youngest of four children born to John Leonade Clare. The oldest was Maggie, then came John and Billy before Archie was born in 1927. John Clare owned several hundred acres in and around Wayfare. He farmed tobacco, cotton, wheat, and beans, and he raised livestock as well. His house stood on a sweet parcel of land of a few hundred acres, about a third of which was covered by a cypress pond. Archie's grandfather had first settled there shortly after the Civil War. Archie calls the house that his grandfather built "the new house." When Archie's father got married, he built a new and larger house at the north end of the pond and moved there to raise his family. Archie, however, spent much of his childhood in the new house, where his father's sisters continued to live. Archie's spinster aunts, Pearl and Rose, enjoyed having children around, and Archie would help them with chores. Several times every day Archie would run down a path between the two houses, a path that threaded its way through whatever grew in that field in a given season: cotton, corn, wheat, soy, or tobacco.

Archie's father was a mule farmer, which means that all of the fieldwork was done with mules, except for some of the heaviest work, which was sometimes done with a team of horses. When Archie was a boy, farming possessed for him the quality of inevitability. Farming was what families in Lothian County did in order to live. Everyone in the family worked in whatever way he or she was able; the same was true for the families of all the boys Archie knew at school. There was hardly any other employment available within the various communities that Archie was familiar with as a boy.

Archie remembers that when he was young everything the world threw his way interested him, but the two most meaningful events of his youth were when he put on a Boy Scout uniform for the first time and when he broke a mule colt—both signals to him that he was growing up. The uniform had already faded by the time he broke the colt, and working like a man in a field far outshone any old suit of clothes, as far as he was concerned. He was eleven or twelve years old, it was June, school had just let out, and the corn and cotton were about three inches tall. Training, or "breaking," a colt to the plow involved teaching it to walk down the middle of a row several rows over from the one where Archie maneuvered the plow. For one entire week Archie plowed one side of each row in the field of corn, and then all the next week he plowed the other side. The black women who worked in the fields moved down the row first to remove the big clumps of weeds and grass. Then Archie followed with a maneuver that was called the "sweep." He trained the colt by pulling, switching, and yelling. Yelling "Gee" moved the mule one step to the right; yelling "Haw" moved it one step to the left. The idea was to teach the mule to drag the plow blade just a few inches from the base of the seedlings in order to clear away weeds and to turn dirt into the top of the row where the seedlings' roots would begin to take hold. Archie plowed this way until the Fourth of July, when the last cultivating was done right down the middle of each row, called "bustin' the middle." While the various workers performed in the field, Archie's father supervised and drove around the field in a car or truck to give them water. Breaking a colt inevitably involved damaging some of the crop, and Archie remembers his father raising hell when he cut too close.

After the middle of July, Archie trained the colt to sled tobacco. The mule dragged a wagon that had rails instead of wheels alongside a tobacco cropper, who cut individual tobacco leaves from the plant and laid them on the sled.

By the time Archie was fifteen years old he was cropping tobacco. Cropping, also called priming or stripping, was hot, miserable work that was particularly rough in the first days when the lowest leaves were cut. Croppers would move up the stalk of the plant as the leaves matured; by the time they were halfway up the stalk, the work had become comparatively easy.

Archie's parents had always figured that education was essential to their children's welfare. Since they weren't born wealthy they would have to get by with hard work and brain power. Archie's mother had graduated from Women's College in Greensboro and had taught high school for several years before she got married. And as Archie remembered, "There was a saying in the forties— 'An education is something nobody can ever take away from you.'" Archie's brother John had finished two years of college at North Carolina State College before going into the service in World War II. John had been in the ROTC and came back to Maxton Airbase to train as a glider pilot; he eventually flew a glider behind enemy lines in France. Billy served in the merchant marines.

After the war, Archie's brothers came home from the service and, as Archie would say, "The whole country was gung ho on education." Archie was already planning to go to college; once he finished high school, and after staying at home and working with his father from June 1945 until the fall of 1946, he entered North Carolina State. As Archie recalls, it was easy to go to college at that time: "You didn't have to be accepted—you just went up and registered for classes, signed up for a dormitory room, and that was all there was to it." There were no entrance requirements or examinations to pass before getting in. Staying in school was a little different, though: "If you didn't have a C average at the end of your first year, they kicked you out."

Archie did not have an easy time studying or making good grades, even though being in college helped to calm the restlessness that was beginning to characterize his adult life. When he entered, North Carolina State was swamped with returning soldiers. The junior and senior classes were swollen to double their normal sizes. Archie's brother John was one of the returning juniors. Archie remembers that State was a hard school back then because the only way to relieve the overcrowding was to make the first years so difficult that those with lower than C averages would have to leave, along with other discouraged students. Archie lived with three other men in a dorm room designed for two. He slept on the top of a three-tier bunk bed and studied at a little card table parked in the corner of the room. He took freshman English, algebra, biology, and classes in his major fields. At a time when the most popular major in college was engineering, Archie first studied textiles then switched after two quarters to general agriculture, which he found much more to his liking. He made some good friends at college. He also played drums in the bugle corps and spent time with his brother John.

But in 1948, after two years at college, Archie left school for a while. He stayed home and farmed with his father. He was planning to return to college in the fall of 1950 when the Korean War started heating up. Archie's father was worried about Archie being drafted into the army and advised him that while he could go back to school if he wanted, he would not be able to receive deferment from the service. Archie decided to sign up for the air force.

When Archie left the farm in Wayfare, his father and mother were still running it. His brother John had finished his B.S. in agriculture, and since there were no other jobs available, he continued farming with his father. John and his father worked well together, and occasionally they would make enough extra money to begin a new venture. The summer before Archie went into the service they had planted a crop of sweet potatoes for the first time. The year before, Archie, John, and their father had purchased some land farther north in the Sandhills. They cleared it, set up a fence around it, and planted it with watermelons, corn, and grain in order to clear the blackjack oak roots out of the ground before putting cattle on the land the following year. Still, Archie could count on one fact of his family's farm economics remaining constant: tobacco provided the only stable income. Every other crop made contributions that were minor in comparison.

During the summer of the year Archie took off from college, he spent several weeks picking up a few credits at Catawba College. He also started dating Waynette McKay, a young woman from Farlanboro who had just finished her sophomore year of college in Charlotte. The social scene included dancing and going to dinner clubs, swimming in the Lumber River and in the millponds, and driving around on the county roads.

Before Archie joined the air force he bought a second-hand 1950 Ford for twelve hundred dollars. Archie drove to Lackland Air Force Base in Florida and began his basic training. Two weeks after arriving he received word that his father had died. He returned to Wayfare for a month's emergency leave, and by the time he got back to Florida all of the people he had met had been sent off to their assignments. Basic training convinced Archie that he wanted to fly a jet, but he couldn't do well enough on the tests to get into flight school. He quickly realized that without flying, life in the service would be tedious. He decided to take every opportunity to go to training schools where he could pick up specialized skills. At least he could learn some new things and see the country at the same time.

The first opportunity was to go to Connelly Air Force Base in Texas to learn about radar. In the fifties the air force was converting from crank power to jet power, and radar technology was being applied in new ways. From November 1951 to June 1952 Archie trained in Texas and flew as a radar operator in B-25s. The training was designed to prepare him to operate radar sets in F-89 fighter-bombers and introduced him to operating the radar during night flying. Archie remembers that much of the training rapidly became obsolete because new and better aircraft were being developed and manufactured almost overnight.

From Texas, Archie went back to Florida, to Elgin Air Force Base and Duke Field, an air proving ground. He tells about working during the hot summer of 1952 as a security guard at the buildings that housed experimental drone aircraft, old B-17s that had been converted to a drone system.

He remembers that it was so hot that the only place he could cool off was in the crawl space beneath the buildings on the base.

Security at the base was tight because the drone system was not only lifesaving, but potentially war-winning experimental technology. The drone aircraft would fly without pilot or crew and would be controlled by another aircraft, the mother ship, from a considerable distance. The mother ship could guide the drone over hostile territory so that it could deliver its bombs without endangering the lives of pilot and crew. Eventually the drone missile would take the place of the drone aircraft, which was never actually used in war.

The drone aircraft became important as a target in the testing of new missiles, however. While Archie was at the base in August, the base commander was flying in the mother ship during such a test over the gulf. The weather was terrible: it was raining hard, the wind was gusting, and the clouds were low. The radar operator picked up the wrong blip in the inclement weather and mistook the mother ship for the drone. Whoever launched the missile from the F-86 sent it toward the mother ship, and it killed the crew and the field commander. The drone must have continued south over the gulf toward South America until it ran out of fuel and dropped from the sky.

From Elgin, Archie transferred to Sumter, South Carolina, where, as he likes to recite, he joined the Sixty-sixth Technical Squadron of the Sixty-sixth Tactical Wing of the Tactical Air Command. His business was reconnaissance. After a month or so he was sent out to Denver, Colorado, to train in air force intelligence. There he learned reconnaissance intelligence, radar mapping, photograph mapping, and interpretation of aerial photographs. He also learned how to ski. After training in Colorado for four months, until March of 1953, he went back to Florida for a month before returning to Sumter. In June of 1953 he shipped out from Charleston for Germany on the USS *General Elting*, a Liberty ship.

Archie remembers the voyage to Germany as uneventful. The ship docked first at New York City but remained only long enough for additional troops to board, and the reconnaissance squadron, along with all the others on board, was not allowed to go ashore. Still, Archie says that he saw all he ever wanted to see of New York from the ship. From New York it took ten days to cross the Atlantic. When the ship docked at Bremerhaven in northern Germany, Archie and his group boarded a train immediately and rode all day and night until they arrived at their post, just outside of Kaiserslautern in the French Zone of West Germany, about forty miles southwest of Frankfort near Worms in the Saar Basin.

The air force's Sixty-sixth Technical Squadron was located in a contonement area, one three-story barracks and a workshop, on an army base. An army field artillery company and a transportation company were also stationed at the base. Breakfast was served from five-thirty to seven in the morning, lunch from twelve to one, and dinner from five-thirty to six-thirty in the evening. Archie's usual workday lasted from eight in the morning until five at night. He was free to leave the base evenings and weekends, but he had to return by ten-thirty each night.

A20-A reconnaissance planes, stationed at an airfield in Sembach, about eight miles away from the base, would run sorties over Germany and neighboring areas in order to take photographs of the land. Archie's crew performed three main functions: they would develop the film, interpret the photographs, and draw maps from them. Archie's job was to interpret the photographs. He would receive a

stretch of about fifty photographs at a time, and he was responsible for observing and identifying anything that could
benefit air force intelligence. He would look for anything
large being transported on roads or by rail, he would study
pictures of factories to determine what they produced, he
would take the measurements of bridges, and so on. Most
of the work did not produce any information of interest or
importance, he recalls, and it mainly served to prepare the
crew for a time when their reconnaissance skills might become valuable. The photograph interpreters used stereoscopes that produced three-dimensional images, and Archie
remembers that often his colleagues would fall asleep with
their heads in their hands as they appeared to be looking
through their scopes.

The highlights Archie mentions from his work in Germany were the time they built an enormous aerial photograph of Liechtenstein on the office wall—which allowed
them to produce curious statistics on sheep and castles—
and the time they received some radar photographs of
Berlin and other East German cities that no one knew how
to interpret. In 1955 Archie and some of his buddies went
on a skiing trip during their leave. They took a train to the
highest mountain in Bavaria, Zugspitze, and rented skis.
The Germans had built a weather station on top that to
Archie looked like a castle. The slopes were icy and the
runs were too difficult for some of the skiers, so they went
to Garmisch and skied a nearby slope where people rode
to the summit in a tram. Archie and his friends stayed in
a pension where they made conversation with a chambermaid who spoke English. When they returned to Kaiserslautern, one of his buddies told Archie that he had been
walking in downtown Garmisch one night when he had
run into the chambermaid on the street. They had a few
beers and then, as the friend told him, they went outside,

crawled into a snowbank, and had a ball. Archie's friend had just come from the doctor, though, who told him that he had returned from Garmisch with more than just the memories.

According to at least one of his air force friends, Archie established himself as the squadron mediator. Archie himself remembers that there were five or six blacks in his squadron. Occasionally racial tensions would surface, and he would try to reason with his white colleagues, a tactic that at least twice got him into trouble. Once when a superior entered the barracks raving about blacks, Archie called him a son of a bitch. It was not so much that Archie had adopted the moral high ground as that the pointless exhibition of anger and hatred annoyed him. And once, when a bunch of the reconnaissance squadron was out on the town they ran into several soldiers who worked at the motor pool on the base. A hotheaded and racist Irishman hit a black motor-pool man over the head with a bottle of gin. When Archie stepped between them, the man who received the bottle of gin slashed Archie's head with a knife.

There weren't many fights and there was little overt racism in the squadron, however, as Archie recalls. But there was drinking. Some members of the squadron were hell-raisers and made a business of barhopping and visiting the professional Fräuleins. The only death in the squadron occurred when a young private who previously had abstained from alcohol was given a vodka punch during a Christmas party. He drank all night, and then passed out on his bunk. He lay on his left arm in such a way that he cut off his circulation, which, when combined with his alcohol intoxication, proved fatal.

Back in Farlanboro, Waynette had begun receiving presents in the overseas mail from the farm boy from Wayfare. Archie sent her bracelets, earrings, china, pictures, and a very few words—but apparently just the right ones.

Waynette had grown up in Farlanboro. Her first memories are of the house she lived in as a girl. It still stands on a back street just a few blocks from downtown, but it has fallen into disrepair. When Waynette was about eight the family moved to a large brick house on Main Street. Her father was a banker in Farlanboro, and her mother's family was in timber. Waynette had gone to Queens College in Charlotte where she majored in French, and she enjoyed every minute of her college life. She had finished college about a year before Archie left for Germany. She returned to Farlanboro where she taught part-time, then full-time, in various high schools. Occasionally she would see Archie when he was on leave, and when Archie was stationed at Sumter, South Carolina, they started to date a couple of weekends every month. But it wasn't until they viewed their relationship from a greater distance, from across the Atlantic, that it started to look serious.

Archie departed from Germany on a troopship that left from Bremerhaven and sailed to New Jersey. He disembarked and took a bus to New Brunswick, where he was stationed until his discharge a week later at the end of August 1954. He then took a plane from Newark to Fayetteville, North Carolina, stopping in Washington, D.C., on the way. He remembers traveling on a Constellation Airlines' four-motor plane with two rudders. Before it landed it approached the airport in D.C. over the Potomac, and Archie saw the Washington Monument for the first time.

Archie had been stationed at seven bases in four years. His moving around slowed his advancement through the ranks, and he left the air force as a buck sergeant instead of a staff sergeant. The military routine had made everything tedious, even visiting parts of the country and the world that he would never have seen otherwise. Neither the work nor the life in the service suited him, and he was glad to be out of it.

/////

When Archie returned to Wayfare, the farm was in trouble, hit by drought and hurt by unsteady management. Archie helped where he could for what was left of the year, but he quickly began to see that staying on the family farm wasn't for him. He was restless and independent. But there weren't any jobs, so he decided to go back to school beginning in January. But first, Archie took a long drive out to Colorado to see some friends from the service. While he was there he decided he'd go back home and marry that woman to whom he'd sent all the presents—if she'd have him. She would, and did.

Archie and Waynette were married in a double-ring ceremony in November 1954 in Farlanboro Presbyterian Church. More than two hundred people attended. After the Friday rehearsal, Archie and Waynette, the wedding party, friends, and family had a cake cutting. At noon on the day of the wedding Waynette's aunts held a luncheon. The wedding took place at five o'clock, and Waynette had five attendants: three cousins, a friend, and her college roommate. Her father gave her away, and Archie's best friend from Wayfare, Joe E. Murray, was the best man. The bridesmaids, maid of honor, and matron of honor wore floor-length dresses of gold taffeta and carried bouquets of bronze chrysanthemums. Waynette describes her own dress almost as if remembering the words of the newspaper account that announced the wedding. She wore a dress of candlelight satin and Alençon lace, with a tight bodice fastened down the back with dozens of tiny covered buttons. The neckline of her dress was high, and she had tight, full-length sleeves and a full skirt that ended in a long train. From her Juliet cap fell a veil of illusion. Waynette's parents gave the reception at their house.

Before going up to Raleigh to enroll for the winter quarter, Archie and Waynette had applied for married student housing, but they didn't receive an opening until one week before Archie graduated. So they found an apartment in downtown Raleigh in the basement of a house owned by an older couple with no children. There were four rooms in all: a living room, a bedroom, a kitchen, and a bathroom. Archie says that there weren't many young career men in the United States during the days when he returned to school. The young men in the service had either been killed or they had gone to college on the GI Bill or they had left the service and college in order to join the 52-20 club—for 52 weeks they could receive $20 a week. Since the government was footing the bill, the university was still full of students. Archie himself received $125 a month, which did not cover expenses, so he took a job in the Department of Economics where he "made book." Making book was the process of assembling a professor's typed lecture and text notes for distribution. The college printing press would print up the papers in sets of twelve unbound double sheets. Archie would place them in a collating machine and then put the various stacks on a large table. Then the student workers would walk around the table and "bip" the pages—pick them up in sequence with wet fingertips.

Waynette also had a job. She worked for the dean of instruction at the School of Agriculture, where she kept student records. When the dean found out that she had been a high school teacher, he made her grade some of the basic agriculture class tests and papers. That was the course that students and administrators called the "weed out course" because only half the students would pass it to continue with the major.

Even with two jobs between them and the GI Bill, Archie and Waynette had so little money that they drove back home every weekend for a few good meals and to get butter and eggs and whatever else their families could give them to take back to Raleigh. Archie stayed in school through the summer and completed the requirements for his degree in agricultural economics within a year and a half. He earned what he terms a good C average, and by his own admission he was never a very good student.

Archie got a job with the Federal Land Bank, a government institution that made low-interest loans to farmers, right at the time he graduated in the spring of 1956. He was an appraiser and would determine the value of whatever property farmers were using as security for the loans they took out with the bank. Archie and Waynette stayed in Raleigh for six months, even though most of Archie's work took him to Lothian County and the Sandhills.

In late 1956 Archie and Waynette moved to Farlanboro. Waynette found a job teaching at a junior high school in a small town west of Farlanboro. After a year, she started teaching French at Farlanboro High School, the town school for whites.

Archie began to collect the old bricks they would use to build their house once they could afford to buy a plot of land. As he traveled through the region he kept his eyes open for old chimneys from burned, fallen, or abandoned homes, and he would return on the weekends with a truck to gather the bricks. The Clares' first child, Catherine McKay Clare, was born in February of 1958, just a few months before the Clares' new house was finished.

In the late fifties and the early sixties farmers could borrow from the Federal Land Bank only 50 percent of the appraised market value of the property and equipment they used for collateral. Since there was no way the federal program could compete with private institutions when the federal bank would only lend up to 35 percent of the money actually required to purchase property, a scaling back of the program became inevitable.

On January 20, 1961, the day John Kennedy was inaugurated, Archie lost his job as an appraiser for the Federal Land Bank due to massive restructuring of the program that reduced the number of state appraisers in North Carolina from eight to two. In one way, Archie was sad to lose his job. The work was interesting, it allowed him to travel around the region, and the money was fair. But in another way, Archie was just as happy to give it up. He found that being an appraiser was not making him any friends, and working for the government was not earning him any points in his community.

/ / / / /

Archie's years away from the farm, away from Lothian County and the idiosyncrasies of a place on the margin of the world, no more removed him from farming than they erased his memory of time and place. Archie had wanted to fly jets, and his inability to do so may have removed the only means by which he could have attained the velocity required to move him out of the sphere of the land and the ways he had known all his life. Wayfare and Farlanboro, and the blank spaces that surrounded them on the map, had been the world to Archie. Farlanboro, were it a bit more picturesque, might be used today by production companies for the settings of their movies about the forties. Archie's travels in the service, his work in Germany, and his stints at North Carolina State College had shown him the real scope of the world and taught him that there were many different ways to live. Archie would never again view farming as the only way to make a living. He had seen that, at certain times and under certain conditions, farming appeared to be simply an anachronism in a new world built by engineers. Archie had seen farming through the eyes of air force sergeants and future accountants at college and saw that it did not occupy a place in their worlds at all. He had seen farming through books, through ink spent in the interest of theory and pragmatics. And he had seen farming from a loftier, quieter, more disinterested perspective than all the others when he had viewed the earth through his stereoscope for hours on end—the earth laid out in fields and woods and towns. A sheep and a stone and a fence and a crop had become equally important and equally insignificant; the personal markings of latitude and longitude became lost in an aesthetic stupor that to Archie's mind resolved the homely particulars of all places into the gray beauty of the everyday. Archie had seen that important events in a life can occur in places where the people who would care are nowhere to be found, at times when nobody seems to pay much attention. A young man from Ohio had gotten drunk and died in his sleep thousands of miles from home, a young German woman had rolled in the snow with a man she would never see again, a father had died while his youngest son was away training during his first weeks in the air force.

When he left the Federal Land Bank in 1961, Archie began to establish the livelihood that would occupy him for almost the next thirty years. In the spring of 1961 he bought a tractor and began to use it to work the fields of farmers he knew in Lothian County. When he could get the work, he would scout timber tracts for lumber companies. He borrowed trucks and logged his wife's land when there were no other jobs. In 1961 the Clares had a son, Robert Alexander, and in 1963 they had another daughter, Anne Leonade.

By 1965 the pattern of his occupation clearly favored farming. He had good years and bad years, but the good balanced out the bad, or so it seemed to him. Over the years the elements that would determine his situation in 1986 began to be assembled even as the circuit of the land he worked became defined. Once the Clares had built their house in Farlanboro, Archie had to do a lot of driving in order to farm. The distance of his farmland from home and the remoteness of the tracts from each other prevented Archie from diversifying. He felt that he couldn't raise livestock because he didn't live close enough to give cows, hogs, or chickens the attention they required. Moreover, a lot of time that might have gone into mending fences, experimenting with new crops, or working with produce was lost in his commuting to the various farms. Living in Farlanboro meant that he would have to find people who would look after his equipment, and that meant additional expense.

As Archie started to farm regularly, he discovered that farming was undergoing a transformation far more subtle than, but at least as significant as, the change from horse to diesel power: the shift from the field to the desktop. Farming was becoming a business of assembling and distributing paper. And the paper that governed his business disguised economic shortfalls by delaying payment and exaggerating prosperity. In the new order of farming a thriving field of wheat could represent devastation as easily as success; an empty field could as often mean profit as loss.

He also learned that the remoteness of his farms and the abstractness of the papers and certificates that accumulated on his desk in any given season only increased his vulnerability to drought. Archie discovered that it was as much sustained frustration as dilution of resources that exposed him to the rigors of weather. This vulnerability couldn't be controlled by fastidious attention to crops or by rigorous application to the papers of farming.

Archie accepted the fact that his brother John would carry on alone the business of the family farm. Maybe it was the complication of the family's economy further pushed by drought, or maybe just the routine intricacies of the farming bureaucracy that led John to make decisions that he could scarcely communicate, let alone make understood. Or maybe it was the deference of the youngest to the eldest son or simply Archie's independent spirit that led him to sever his business ties with his brother. When he had resolved to go off on his own, Archie gave up his share of the house and the family land immediately surrounding it in order to ensure that his brother Billy would have a place to live after their mother died. Billy had grown quite eccentric since the war and was finding it impossible to apply himself to work. He lived in the new house with his mother and seldom left it.

Having quit the family farm and without the capital necessary to purchase land, Archie had to come by acreage however he could and make the best of whatever he could scrape together. What little money he had saved while working for the Land Bank went into a down payment for a tractor. That's why he started off farming Waynette's family's land: it was available and he could use some for free and the rest at a discount. One tract of it, the Sinclair farm, divided by one of the major highway routes to the Carolina shore, was composed of fifty-eight cleared acres, seventy in Bootheel Swamp wooded with pine, oak, gum, poplar, and cypress, and thirty on the rise and across the highway from the swamp, some of it also wooded. Just off the highway at the Sinclair farm was an old house that had been in various stages of repair and disrepair over the years. A hundred yards away from the house stood a grain silo and the barn that would house most of Archie's equipment: his John Deere tractor, his International Harvester combine, his truck for hauling, and his various hitches. Some of whatever profits came off the farm were devoted to maintaining the land and buildings. A percentage of the profits, when there were any, went to Waynette, principal owner of the land. The other tract he farmed, the Glencairn farm, had eighty acres cleared and seventy in woods; it belonged to Waynette's brother, a banker who lived in Fayetteville and who in winter occasionally hunted bird there. Archie owned twenty-five acres outside Wayfare—property that had come down to him from his father—but he rarely farmed it himself and usually rented it to his brother John. Wayfare, ten miles north of Farlanboro and more than twenty miles from the Sinclair farm, was too far away from Archie's base of operations to make farming it himself worthwhile.

By 1986, Archie generally worked about 215 acres each year, 6.5 of it growing his tobacco allotment of 11,500 pounds, the profits from which he, his wife, and his brother-in-law split. In addition to tobacco, he rotated corn (sweet and field), soybeans, and winter wheat on the land. Most years he grew produce, melons, and cantaloupes, which some years he sold from a highway stand right on the farm. He did try hogs a couple years, but he found that they required too much attention. And he did try cotton in an almost nostalgic gesture to the days when cotton was still king, but he found that the mills wouldn't pay well for Lothian County cotton, which tended to have shorter fibers than the cotton grown farther to the south and southwest. Perhaps if he'd had more land and more reliable labor cotton would have done well for Archie.

Two hundred acres is just about the limit of what one man can work alone, Archie says. But the isolation of the different tracts he farmed began to strain his resources when the bad years overbalanced the good. When he took into account where he bought fuel, fertilizer, and seed, where he dealt with the bank, the government, and the combine mechanics, where he took the tobacco to market and bought his own produce, and the distance he had to drive just to get to one of the farms and back, he realized that he had undertaken the business of broadcasting weeds on a windy day. Maybe it was his experience as an interpreter of aerial photography that led him to describe his farming operation the way military historians account for the movement of forces at the battle of Gettysburg. The physical facts of Archie's business, the geographical axioms, can be described as a circuit, a circuit he drove every day, sometimes several times a day, a circuit of land, activity, and resources whose connections were maintained only by Archie's driving, only by his creating a system out of places that for his purposes were as far-flung as satellites.

TWO

WE CROUCHED in the shade of the truck on a rutted dirt road in Campbell County and surveyed the crop. It looked like death as much as life grew in the fields. As Archie stepped from the truck and crouched, summer tipped its hat. Eighty acres of corn withered as Archie lit his cigarette. Rows of tobacco blistered as he shifted his hat to shade his eyes. As he scratched his chin, all the moisture in three counties dissolved into dust inside melons that hid under leaves wilted to the softness of ashes. Discontentment has a way of easing into thought the way the chalk dust of white heat settles over a stand of pines and smudges the corners of the horizon. It settled on his face as stubble—a finely ground dust of what might have been, a grainy residue of chemicals, curses, and sweat.

First stop of the morning. It was Friday, July 11, and by ten o'clock I had already had too much of the single most constant fact of Archie's work: life in the truck. For most of the year, whenever he shifted the engine into gear his mind had time to idle. But in that morning's ninety-five-degree heat he required all of his energy just to stay awake and hold the wheel, just to distinguish in sounds memories of the self, just to reaffirm that he and the truck were distinct, that he was moving in the world and that the trees, fields, and roads were not a dream. This was the kind of morning that would keep Archie Clare from talking. This was the kind of heat that made even Archie conserve his energy. And what Archie saw left him very little to talk about, even if he had been able to find the words.

Archie saw that there was not a thing to do in that field. In the drought the earth itself appeared to have shriveled up. There was nothing but the inert sand, parched tobacco leaves lofting their fragrance over the soil as they burned slowly in the sun, a whiff of asphalt, a hint of crows, and the memory of a dog in a ditch. Archie climbed back into the truck, poked his ribs for another smoke, stuck it in his mouth and lit it, and turned the key in the ignition. He slowly circled the field, arm stuck out the window, directing the truck by jerking the wheel as he gazed wordlessly at the crop.

On the other side of the road from where the stunted tobacco and field corn wasted away stood his tobacco barns. Next to the road was an old stick barn that Archie no longer used; its aged boards looked pliable as leather. Not more than a hundred feet beyond the stick barn stood two new aluminum bulk barns, set down end to end like two mobile homes. A hundred yards down the road from the barns was an old house with walls the color of dirtied eggshells just pulled from the clutch. When Archie stopped the truck and we climbed out, a pair of turkey vultures circled each other and sank below a line of trees at the back of the property. Archie ignored the tobacco and field corn on the other side of the road and concentrated on the sweet corn that grew in the field behind his tobacco barns— about a quarter acre of Silver Queen between the smaller of the two bulk barns and the old house. We waded over the dead furrow, then walked through the thin green shanks and rough-grained leaves. Archie stopped and ripped open a truncated ear and found it blistered. Squatting between rows of corn I looked up through the green, through so many promises. Looking down I saw black rot and blue mold swelling the tip of an ear at my knee, a tumorous growth bulging from a stalk behind me. Green beetles scurried about exposed roots. This was only the family's sweet corn—little money had been plowed into it, and even less expectation. There would be enough corn for the table, whether it came from Campbell County or Florida. We stood and walked back to the truck. We climbed into the bitter warm smell of radiator overspill and the bleak shades of nicotine stippled into the upholstery. The drone of the engine was all but drowned out by a blaze of cicadas.

One reason Archie preferred too little to too much rain was that the firmness of droughty fields allowed him to drive right up to the crop. Drought gave him the illusion that there could be something meaningful in driving around. For my part, the heat and the smoke and the blur of the land-scape were making my head spin. After checking the corn we circled back to town to get a battery that had been charging at Phillip's service station, south of Farlanboro. This meant retracing our route through the circuit. As we headed back out of town, south on Highway 151, out from under arching willow oaks and pecans, past produce stands, barns, and roadside shrines, Archie remained silent. Who knows what crossed his mind as we drove? If a mind tends toward its immediate surroundings then his would be con-sidering the bitter smoke of Camels, the hum of tires on the highway, the way a roadbed has of tilting from side to side like a snake in motion. Maybe he envisioned next Hallow-een's jack-o'-lanterns shriveling in their beds, etched with the wrinkled grin of drought.

We passed James Station, where huge dead oaks, many of them twisted into splinters, outline the sites of houses torn up by last year's tornadoes. This small community formed at a crossroads on the former site of the train stop at the James farm. The Jameses had been a prominent family that until the fifties had owned, farmed, and logged thousands of acres in southern Lothian County for several generations. Unused railroad tracks and words on a sign were all that remained to mark the Jameses' tenure on the land. Beyond James Station the highway dropped into swamp, where it was squeezed by small concrete bridges, where we hoped that we wouldn't pass a car, where last winter a pickup smashed into the bridge side. Rising out of Bootheel Swamp we approached the Sinclair farm, the second point on the circuit. Archie slowed, turned, and the traffic stacked up behind us sped on toward the coast, a hundred miles down the road.

/ / / / /

We had set out that morning to see Archie's farming operations. When we found the crop at the first field too disappointing to discuss, Archie had moved on to the next regular stop, the Sinclair farm.

The tenant family there—Dan L. Cooper, Auntie Jess, their daughter Sudi Jane, and her sons Jeeter, Cooter Tom, and Joey—have lived at the Sinclair farm ever since the previous tenants, Preacher Jake McCoy and his wife, Mattie, died. Jake, a minister of the African Methodist Episcopal Zion church, set whatever precedent there was for a black man to live in that section of the county. He was living there long before Archie and Waynette were married and continued to live there until 1976, when he died at the age of ninety-nine. Since it was at the Sinclair farm that Archie stored his tractor, hauling truck, combine, and other gear, he wanted someone living there to keep an eye on things. (After Jake McCoy died, and before Archie had found new tenants to take his place, someone stole Archie's hauling truck.) Jake McCoy was hard to replace: he'd had complete integrity and had gotten along with everyone. His only drawback had been that he had loved to talk Bible to the point that visitors found it hard to keep any conversation short. Dan L.'s family had come from Georgia in the early seventies and had originally arranged with Archie to stay in the house on the Glencairn farm near Archie's tobacco barns. Archie thinks that they had come in hope of Dan L.'s finding work at one of the canneries that had just been built on the western edge of Campbell County. After a couple of years they left the area until, in 1977, they reappeared and Archie suggested that they move into McCoy's old place.

It soon became clear that Dan L.'s family was reclusive and troubled. They kept to themselves and stayed away from the folks on neighboring farms. While Dan L., Auntie Jess, Sudi Jane, Jeeter, and Cooter Tom contributed materially to the prosperity of the farm by working some of the crops and by keeping an eye on the equipment, they also introduced many complications into Archie's business of getting by. For one, they were the only black family living in an area dominated by Indians. That made for a greater likelihood of violence against the farm equipment or property. And then there were the intricacies of dealing with welfare. If Dan L. and Sudi Jane earned too much money it could threaten their payments. Archie couldn't, for example, simply give them an old car to drive around in. He had to keep any such car in his name. They received wages for their work with the crop, and in exchange for a place to live, they kept an eye on the tractor, truck, and combine. Jeeter learned to drive the tractor and would drive the truck occasionally. Some years Archie split the farm's garden produce with Dan L., Archie having cultivated and planted, Dan L. having taken care of the rest, then selling it where he could, either at the farm's roadside stand or to other marketers.

According to Archie, men strolled into Sudi Jane's life like spring weather and departed like frost in sunlight, without ever seeming to leave their names behind. Her son

Cooter, nine years old, was nicknamed for his love of turtle meat. Jeeter, fifteen, was the talker in the family. Joey was five, and while I never actually saw him, at times I could hear him laughing or squalling inside the house.

That day, Sudi Jane sat on the porch, rocking, saying it was a hot morning. Archie went inside to find Dan L. The walls of the eighty-year-old house were paper thin, just thick enough to trap and incubate heat. Boards of the porch floor, polished by wear to a bright dusty enamel, bent with each step. Next to the house stood a crooked basketball goal whose rim drooped down against the backboard. Jeeter says that when he grows up he wants to play in the NBA. Cooter wants to dance ballet.

Archie had come to talk about a station wagon he was thinking about buying for them. Though they couldn't buy a car without the welfare people finding in it some illegitimate source of income, Sudi Jane needed a car to find work. The year before, Sudi Jane's sister, who had been visiting for months, had driven off in their station wagon. Days later she was found dead in a ditch, the car abandoned in a field some five hundred yards away. Someone had stolen the battery and wheels.

Archie and Dan L. emerged from the house. Dan L. was six feet six inches tall. He walked and stood with his chin tucked into his chest and his right ear tilted toward his shoulder, as if he were constantly listening for words from a world of short people. I would eventually notice that Archie was usually reluctant to linger inside Dan L.'s house and preferred to conduct business outside, even in the hot sun. They walked down the steps, the dry sticks of the quince and forsythia raking Dan L.'s arm as he descended. Dan L. said that he didn't know what he could do with Jeeter. He was running up phone bills, talking back. Archie recommended discipline, work, a belt. I could see in Dan L.'s

strange hazel eyes that he was tired—tired of work, tired of
the boys, tired of the heat. He would be sixty-five in a
couple of years and he no longer had what it takes to raise
a teenager. He must have been thinking that Archie knew
damn well there wasn't any work that summer because of
the drought, that it was precisely that lack of work causing
the problems with Jeeter. Dan L. led Archie to the side of
the house where the chopping block stood against a back-
drop of struggling sunflowers. They walked over wood
chips that had turned gray. Dan L. continued talking once
they were far enough away so that their words couldn't be
followed by anyone else.

Sudi Jane still sat, arms flopped over the side of her rocker,
face bent forward in enigmatic scrutiny. Her limbs seemed
asleep, her dress helplessly limp, so thin it could assume no
shape of its own but wrapped her body like a second skin
of sweat. Her face was eager with an intelligence in strange
contrast to her body's disorder. She sat in the shade of the
old white house whose paint had cracked and chipped
away from the worn gray boards of its walls. The gloom of
the porch was overcast by a broad willow oak. Sudi Jane
clicked her tongue and raised her chin. Corn rustled in a
breeze behind the house. Down by the pond crows and
grackles rattled and whistled in briars and thistles. In her
hands Sudi Jane held a white paper napkin that was knot-
ted and shredded. She gripped the ends the way one would
hold clipping shears, or reins. Overhead an airliner's con-
trails fanned in the sky like silt.

In the middle of the yard the willow oak parceled out
thin shade from the precincts of light; below, its roots divided the yard into wedges. Framed by gum and poplar,
the barn beside the creek cast its shadow over the tractor,
truck, and combine across the yard. Out nearer the road,
on the opposite side of the driveway from the house, stood

the produce stand. Between the house and the barn a cylindrical grain bin, unused for years, broke the view from the house to the cornfield. An unattached disk, an old Case drag bar, and an International Harvester cutter-bar mower assembly, its teeth grown dull with rust, were gathered into a mound. Sparse grass crept up between and around them. Off to the side an old moldboard plow rested its colter and yoke against the hollow throats of several tires piled in a leaning stack. Used and unused, the machinery seemed to whir about the house, to dance and drop just as corn and wheat rose and fell in fields around the nucleus of the house.

Archie had bad news for Dan L. and Sudi Jane could smell it. There was still no work for Jeeter, and, come August, if the tobacco crop turned out as disastrously as it seemed it must, Jeeter wouldn't even have cropping that year. Archie had more bad news than Sudi Jane suspected. The tractor's battery had been stolen again. Jeeter would probably be accused of the theft, and that would almost certainly provoke his restlessness and Dan L.'s fury.

I leaned against the truck and opened a beer. When Sudi Jane asked if I had another beer I gave her one. Embedded in the dry ground at the foot of the porch hundreds of gum tree seedballs opened their many mouths like little bird beaks. There wasn't a gum tree within two hundred yards. Cooter came out of the house and twirled in the sand, his hazel eyes flashing. His brother followed and, watching him, tucked his chin into his shoulder, cocked his elbow and flapped his hand, limp at the wrist. When Archie and I drove off, I looked back and saw Cooter toss Dan L.'s hat into the air and catch it on his head, perfectly centered.

"You shouldn't have given Sudi Jane that beer," Archie said. We pulled past Clark's Grocery after crossing Bootheel Creek. "She shouldn't be drinking. Neither should

Dan L." He turned left at a crossroad and was headed back toward Glencairn farm. "Of course, you couldn't have known that."

We took a series of turns that placed us on a projection into Campbell County, driving along roads through stretches of pine and field that it was hard to imagine anyone having any use for. Such a drive will convince you that a human is a fragmentary consciousness stuck to a bundle of sticks, that will and intelligence were never designed to operate above forty-five miles per hour or eighty-five degrees Fahrenheit. Morning had turned the corner from purgatory to eternal heat, and it was noon. Archie had lit another Camel, and I couldn't imagine where we were going, since we'd already checked on both the farms. Another stop became a dreaded certainty. Fifteen minutes away from Sudi Jane's porch we pulled off the road, down a long, sandy driveway. Archie had remembered that Waynette wanted him to pick up some field peas for dinner, so he had headed over to George's. George was a young farmer who lived in Campbell County and helped Archie with his farms on occasion. George maintained a fine garden of greens, field peas, and tomatoes. Archie stopped the truck suddenly and started backing out of the driveway. He pointed out that you always know a farmer isn't home when his truck is gone.

/////

Air-conditioning wheezed through the vents of the house. Archie's circuit naturally looped back to his home on the west edge of town. After he had done all he could do at the farms, after he had picked up whatever produce there was along the way, after he had looked at his parched crops and checked in with Auntie Jess and Dan L., he would stop at the house for a nap before heading to the Lumber River in the afternoon. It would be fair to say that what Archie

missed most about living in Wayfare on the family farm
was proximity to the river. During the summer in Lothian
County, people seem to orient themselves by estimating their
distance from the Lumber.

Heading north toward Wayfare somehow seemed easier
than heading south and east to Sinclair and Glencairn. The
road appeared to rise, and parcels of land and forest seemed
statelier. Trees appeared thicker to the north and, oddly
enough, bluer. We crossed railroad tracks on Turnpike Road.
To the right a large field of cotton stretched all the way to
the bypass. To the left a house and barn whose once red
paint had been turned to gray by the sky clustered a few
hundred yards from the highway, and the fields around
them were covered with straw-colored weeds. Our view
of the fields was cut by woods as the road veered east. A
sparrowhawk perched on an electric line. We passed an old
church where, Archie told me, Sherman's troops had stopped
and camped during their journey north, carving their ini-
tials on the bell tower walls and tearing out pews to bridge
a nearby creek. We crossed Highway 151 and hit 49, which
runs northeast to the Lumber River and Drew County beyond Wayfare. We passed pines and oaks and occasional
swampy stands of gum bordered with poplar. I counted
timber rattlers dead on the road. We turned onto another
highway. Above us the sky glowed white.

The road rose and we saw pine; it fell and we found
hardwood. Open land held field corn, unblooming cotton,
some early soybeans, the stubble of winter wheat in fields
where farmers had decided not to plant. And tobacco, dor-
mant, waiting for rain. When road signs led me to antici-
pate a town, we would pass only a crossroads with a gas
station or a small bungalow featuring yard statuary for
sale. Satellite dishes stood in front of even the most dilapi-
dated homes. Occasionally huge old farmhouses, invari-

ably built of wood, crowned small elevations or sat nestled among shade trees in the middle of their fields. We passed innumerable old wooden tobacco bulk barns, like Archie's own stick barns: stolid block buildings with single-gabled roofs. Typically they had a single door; those still in use had tin awnings jutting from the roof above the entry. These buildings are called stick barns, from the sticks used to hold the tobacco during curing. Several tobacco leaves are wrapped together and tied at the stems with string and then tied to two-by-two wooden sticks, which are then laid across wooden crossbars that ascend nearly to the roof of the barn. Occasionally we passed the new and expensive aluminum bulk barns. These barns, which look like squared-off silver Airstream trailers, have electric fans and heat sources for controlled curing.

Above us the sky all but disintegrated. Sunlight flaked off of the great dome and fell in mind-numbing sheets. In the truck, conversation flagged. Never having gotten off to a decent start, it now sputtered between Archie's cigarettes. Outside, insects whirred in the machinery of the season. Pines and oaks dreamt of rain. The radiator clicked. Archie lit a cigarette. As he would have said, the tobacco worked slow death in his hands, his bones, his shins, and his bank account—even as he tried to turn the land into the smoke he breathed. That day the ground had little moisture to yield, and what there was had risen at dawn and had begun working on our shirts the second we stepped outside the house. It had gathered itself aloft after noon into fluffy white false hopes and drifted toward the coast to rain on someone else's land. It hadn't rained on any of Archie's land in seven months. Storms flew by overhead, searching for someplace to waste their bounty. Open truck windows and buffeting wind provided no relief. The motor hummed. Tires hissed. After hours of it we had grown too weary to be surprised that we could survive it. On an open stretch of road that ran uninterrupted through fields a ways south of Wayfare, enveloped in the dimness of our cloud of probability, the cigarette went out and we ran out of gas.

"Wait here," Archie said.

/////

Running out of gas was a conspicuous reminder of the drought. The exhaustion of the truck's fuel, combined with the dearth of conversation, functioned like the multiplication of negative integers and led to words. As the truck coasted to a stop Archie pulled it over to the side of the road. His mood had softened and it seemed as though he had derived new energy from the prospect of having a definite problem to solve. He commented almost cheerfully on the sky's shade of blue and mused aloud about the capacity of the truck's fuel tank. At the moment when exasperation thawed his tongue and humanized the landscape, Archie took off.

"I'll walk on up to Will Scott's."

It is hard to imagine anything I would have dreaded more than running out of gas on a July afternoon on a flat road in the middle of nowhere with the temperature over a hundred. Nothing to drink in the truck and the sky cursing the earth with all its power deepened the grimness of the light. I climbed out of the truck and looked ahead as Archie walked up the road. While I could not see any house in the direction that he had headed, clumps of trees about three-quarters of a mile up the road marked what I assumed was his destination.

On July afternoons in Lothian County everything seems to conspire toward the undoing of attention. Hordes of insects fill the air and send up a roar almost as overwhelming as the sunlight. The same noise that on warm summer nights can almost be mistaken for bathwater running, that seems to massage one's limbs with a sensation as delicious as wisteria, is during the heat of the day grating and oppressive. As I stood on the road, the buzz of cicadas lashed out like a live electrical wire. Whatever substance it is in asphalt that gleams like mica flakes made the road look like it possessed its own source of heat and suggested the glistening scales of a snakeskin. On the right-hand side of the highway was a field of corn that looked as dry as it would normally become in September.

The heat radiating from the highway was unbearable, and I looked for shade. Across the road and back thirty yards or so a stand of trees loomed over an old yard that remained clear of underbrush. As I approached the trees I saw that they shaded a concrete walkway and a small house. Swarms of gnats wavered in the beams of sunlight that penetrated the canopy of oak to dapple the roof and walls of the house. The windows and the door had been boarded up, and the entire exterior was covered by wood siding so weathered that small black lines had formed around cells in the wood grain like the craquelure of an old oil painting. Swallows, wasps, and dirt daubers had left the eaves full of their mud and paper houses, even where the wood of the overhanging roof had rotted and left the rusted tin exposed.

The sound of a car horn called me back from that tranquil spot, and when I turned back to the road I saw Archie wave to me from a large blue Cadillac. If we had to run out of gas on a back road in Lothian County, we might as well have done it just down the way from Will Scott's. Will had realized long ago that his farm was too far from the nearest filling station to do him any good, so he had installed a gas tank in his yard. When Will and Archie drove up, I expected them to have a can of gas. But they didn't. They had come to pick me up because, of course, it was so hot. I had a feeling that someone running out of gas just down the road, and not just someone but a cousin, was an interesting event to Will Scott. As we drove to his farm I realized that the clump of trees that had defined the horizon just three-quarters of a mile down the road did in fact harbor Will's house. The dirt and gravel driveway circled the wooden Victorian house, which sat in the midst of several old barns and outbuildings, stands of pecans and willow oaks, and fields of dying corn.

When lives are wound together tightly for a while, when they meet at critical junctures time and time again, a determined familiarity governs all of their subsequent meetings no matter how many miles or years have intervened. Archie and Will were fixtures in each other's minds. They didn't need to visit often anymore or even meet at all. The actions we performed that day—finding the gas can, starting the pump, filling the can with gas, spilling a third of the gas down the truck's side—assumed the air of repeated ritual. This had happened so many times that once more simply seemed appropriate. We talked only of heat. All the things that had passed before—the births and deaths, the failures and successes, the fine cotton and sweet corn that defined their experience and placed them in the same terrain—remained unnoted in our conversation.

When we fetched a gas can from the barn, Will handed Archie his keys and said, "I think that bronze one is the right key, but I'm not sure." Will was an old man and moved with an old man's deliberate gait. He raised his feet the way a chicken does when strutting, and his bones seemed bound together by invisible wires. Each wrist was wired to the knee below it so that his forearms and knees rose and fell in sync. His was the ennobled gauntness of clean living that age had withered to a spit.

After Will filled the gas can, we rode in his Cadillac back to the El Camino, the gas sloshing about and a fine spray of it oiling my arm as I held the can out the car window. Once the El Camino's engine turned over, I drove it to Will's and pulled up alongside the pump. He turned it on and dispensed five gallons into the truck. Archie asked him how he was feeling, and Will said that something was wrong with him and he could go any day. Will was finding it hard to breathe, and the hottest summer he could remember wasn't helping. Later, as we drove toward Wayfare, Archie told me that Will had almost died one day at dinner, that his throat had tightened up on him and he had nearly choked.

"Will Scott is a teetotaler. He used to smoke cigarettes, but as far as I know he never took a drink. Will had lots of land. He inherited a whole lot from his uncle, Old Man Tommy as he was called, who was in the mercantile business. Old Man Tommy bought and sold cotton and other products, and, as they said, his business was to make money. When he died he left his business and his money to Will. Will continued the business and tried to increase it as a young man in the thirties and forties. As he grew older and the tenant system folded up he even tried mechanization. He went to tractors, but he wasn't made that way. He didn't have a knack for it. So he started selling land rather than go into debt. He sold practically all of it. He educated his children. He became county commissioner and served on the school board. He did some political work and had some clout with the Democratic party."

Archie paused and thought for a moment, then continued. "I believe that he was an electoral-college delegate. Will did a lot to get the hospital going and to establish good schools, back in the days when the government was willing to put a lot into the community. He never did a lot of the farming himself, with his own hands, but then he wasn't raised with machinery and wasn't a mechanic. He was primarily a cotton broker. Had a cotton gin. Finally he sold the gin, because of the unreliability of cotton. Cotton's a funny crop—it'll go in spurts. Make money for a few years, then starve you. Mostly the problem is with the prices going down. Cotton likes wet land. Drought will kill it. A cotton gin is the most movable thing in the Southeast."

"What do you mean?" I asked. I had never seen a cotton gin and figured that if it was the size of a combine there would be nothing remarkable about moving one. If it was much bigger it might be worth seeing one moved.

"What I mean is that the cotton gin is the most movable thing in the Southeast in the sense of industry. As long as there was cotton being grown in an area and it looked like there would continue to be cotton grown there, you'd keep the gin. But you could disassemble it and move it." Archie pointed to a barn we were passing.

"That's about the size of a cotton gin," he said. "As far as industrial machinery was concerned it was movable. Not as easily moved as a small sawmill like the kind Waynette's granddaddy used to move around down in Campbell County, but easily enough to give a cotton farmer some flexibility. And, of course, a cotton farmer could single-handedly depress a neighborhood by moving his gin away, and that sort of thing did happen.

"I suppose I wouldn't have had much to do with Will if it weren't for drought. Or cotton gins. When I came home from Germany, that fall right before I got married, it was Will who helped me get started. I had decided to go my own way, to split off from the family farm, and that was partly because of the sad shape that farm was in due to drought. Will put me to work on his uncle's cotton gin.

"Drought," Archie continued after a pause. (I noticed that when Archie said "drought," he sometimes pronounced that last group of consonants "th.") "I didn't know what it meant at first, when I was a kid growing up. I remember in the early thirties we saw the dust rise up out of the west. The sun set red every night, much redder than you see it these days. What we were seeing was the Dust Bowl drought, when the soil west of the Appalachians was so dry that the wind just blew it away and carried it up into the atmosphere. Then drought came again in the seventies, after America had planted corn from fencerow to fencerow in order to sell it overseas. Cultivating all the available land in the country was not a bad idea, and it paid off, economically." He crouched forward, holding the wheel with his elbows as he lit his Camel.

"But it didn't pay off as well as it might. For that was the beginning of the dry years. All that prairie land they put back in corn. Texas. Kansas. Nebraska. The country had bad drought in the thirties. Then the country had it bad in the year Nixon wanted to do away with the gold standard. It was seventy-two, I believe. *Our* drought, the Southeast's drought in seventy-nine I mean, lasted all summer long. Had another in eighty."

"What's the difference between the drought of the thirties and the droughts of the seventies?" I asked.

"I suppose that you'd say the thirties drought was like any other—it was the consequence of too little moisture in the soil and no rain. It turned into a problem of erosion, though, when all the good soil, the topsoil with the nutrients in it, blew away. Then when rain did come there was a similar problem of the soil washing away. But the element of that drought determined by the weather was a fluke, it was freakish. That's the difference, in my opinion, between the droughts early on in the century and the droughts after World War Two. When the big push was on in the fifties, sixties, and seventies to utilize all the land that was available, and the banks were all pushing their loans on farmers who never should have been able to secure loans, all the clearing of land *contributed* to the dry weather. There weren't any trees or other plants to hold in moisture, and often it's moisture on the ground that boils up in summer heat to make rain.

"In seventy-eight the rest of the country, the Midwest especially, had drought. The livestock farmers were forced to sell off big herds of cattle because there was no hay. Farmers in the Southeast baled all the ground cover that we had available—beans, weeds, and hay—and sent it to the Midwest to feed the cattle. The midwesterners were in bad shape. Then in 1980 drought was on top of us. I cut eighty bushels off of fifty-eight acres—a yield of like seven or eight bushels per acre when I should have gotten twenty-five to thirty.

"Daddy himself had bad years in the thirties. I was six or seven and, oh, there were years when we didn't make anything, crops or money. But then, back then you didn't have to buy what you needed to survive. We had our own meat. We had our own horsepower and mules. Oh, we did buy some stuff to increase the fertility of the soil—mostly acid lime. Lime, dirt, and acid mixed together. That's what we used and the soil still wasn't any good. Yields back then were lousy. Twenty-five bushels per acre. One-half bale of cotton per acre. The hand picking of cotton was more efficient, though. Now you see a field of cotton machine picked and it looks like acres of snow melting in the weeds. But back then the sharecroppers—most of them colored— got half of the crop, so they gave a damn about what happened to it. They would pick a little early, then go back later and clean up. Later, in February or March, they'd do what we call 'scrapping' just before the next season's planting—they'd pick up the ragged leftovers. Gathering snow.

They might bring in as much as two bales and earn enough money to plant their own gardens. Some farmers left the scrap for fertilizer, and then a lot liked to gather the cotton scraps in November, in order to buy clothes for winter."

We passed a state prison a few miles outside of Wayfare. Our original plan—to pick up a canoe at Archie's brother John's house and paddle down the Lumber River—had changed after we had run out of gas. We would forget the boat and go straight to the river.

"Our present drought started in the winter of last year," Archie continued. "Eighty-five we're talking about. Come November last year, about the end of the month, a hurricane from the gulf bullied its way inland and that is the last rain we had. The ground stayed wet until mid-January. Seven or eight inches of rain it was, a tremendous amount. The moisture stayed in the soil being as it was winter. The reason I remember is that I had beans to cut for someone, and I damn near buried the combine in mud four or five times. Your farmer hates too much rain. Yes, that was the last good saturation of the soil, and awfully close to the last rain we've had, period.

"Well, then we went on with the year. We had enough moisture in the soil from that big late fall rain to germinate seed. But we haven't had any rain since. Within twenty miles of the Campbell County farm, east, they're having a normal season, and then again, for a hundred miles west they're having drought. Of course, drought ought to affect your planting, but you aren't planning on a drought, so you go ahead with your regular routine of planting during March and April. As I say, in March and April there was enough moisture to germinate the seeds and get them up. Even though it hadn't rained since November. You just go ahead with it when there is no way to predict whether you should or not. You just do it."

He slowed as we entered Wayfare.

"Winter wheat had already suffered a fifteen-bushel reduction in yield. We had ten bushels per acre when normally we would have had twenty-five to thirty. Wheat came off the last of May, first of June. On tobacco you use water anyway as you plant, so we put the tobacco crop in and it was started. But by the time we transplanted the tobacco drought had already set in, and the tobacco grew a little and then stopped. Tobacco grows some in drought, but not much. One thing about a tobacco plant—it will sit there and root normally without water even though you won't find regular leaf growth in drought. If it rains in August then the leaves will grow again, but the quality will be poor and it will be hard to cure. We can still make our poundage, but we will lose the quality. This summer it's looking like the tobacco won't have a chance to ripen. They say—and they're right—that tobacco will wait for rain. So, one sure thing about tobacco: it's like a baby and always seems to be hurting more than it is."

Archie threw a smoking cigarette out the window, looked over at me, and said, "The question is, how long can your farmer wait? Rain will fall, eventually. Has to. But return on a farmer's crop, that's a different story. Debt will only wait so long. One more year of debt may be more than I can stand. If the weather doesn't break this drought it may break me. One thing about your farmer: he's usually hurting more than he seems to be."

//////////////////////

THREE

WAYFARE is a town that never ripened. Near the river, intersected by a spur of the railroad, it seems a place likely to grow, an unlikely town to have died. But whatever promise Wayfare possessed withered and the town along with it, all but its glossy green magnolias. A grocery in a two-story building the upper floor of which was empty, its windows all broken, a vegetable stand, a gasoline station, a used-furniture store, a clothing store in a converted filling station across the street, a dozen empty brick and wood buildings— all are arranged along the street like empty insect shells lined up against a radiator.

As we drove through town toward the river, Archie's conversation turned to people who had lived around Wayfare when he was growing up. He seemed to remember people the way he had remembered the Dust Bowl drought, which he believed he had actually seen in the red sky at sunset when he was a boy. Maybe he had. He told the stories as if the broadest gestures of their lives revealed their private motives and desires. He talked as if his accounts of lives lived could somehow fill in the void left by drought in the middle of the growing season.

"There was an old woman who lived above Clay Bank," he began. "Well, you'll see where she lived, up in the wilderness you might say. Away from everybody else, at least ten miles from the road. She'd had a husband. The road that runs up there was used for wagon-teams. Of course, you could go either way on the river, up or down, so she had that too. She was an old colored woman who lived there by herself after her husband died. Well, she was old when I saw her as a little boy. My father and one of his friends wanted to get out and look around one day up here in the Sandhills, and they took me with them. You might say Daddy loved to ramble. I was riding with him, and if I remember right we'd already been to the swimming hole at Clay Bank before we went out the other end of the road way on up in the Sandhills where we saw her homesite. She and her husband owned a mule, a one-horse wagon, and they'd come to town with them every once in a while. With the mule they planted vegetables. Also had hogs. They didn't need to buy anything. There wasn't any Social Security. Wasn't any welfare. After the old man died, I guess the old lady probably lived on what people gave her as far as money goes. The rest, her livelihood, came from whatever she could scare up in the woods. Wasn't anywhere for her to spend money anyway. How she got up there in the first place I don't know. I don't think they owned the land. They probably just wandered by and sat down and never did leave, you know. But why, I don't know—she wasn't benefiting anybody but herself. She enjoyed not having to mess with any of it. You know. The world. Society. Money."

We had turned off the Wayfare highway about one-half mile before the Lumber River and now proceeded down an old road whose blacktop had buckled into a chaos of ripples and fragments. To the left lay a huge field that had recently been logged. To me the woods looked uninhabitable, but it was becoming apparent that Archie felt at home on this remote sand road and that he recognized in the shadows of the trees and fields a human presence that I could scarcely glimpse. He saw another world superimposed upon the one I saw. His words revealed the extent to which the world of the living was connected to the world of the dead, and his narratives negotiated between the objects of his memory and his imagination. The trees became the medium of an exchange that transformed an inert land-scape into a living fabric: heat and sunlight turned the trees into an aquifer that communicated the runoff of many years back to the mind again, the disconnected and fragmented memories of absent actions, things, and words.

The land under the pines in the Sandhills is so poor, the saying goes, that it only serves to hold the world together. Yet the long road to Clay Bank traverses land that works on the mind like a spell: dry and dusty, reflecting light from waxy leaves in scrub oak woods, every shadow becomes a hive of bugs, and coiled round every tuft of wire grass is a snake. Archie saw in the woods and fields, the way one sees light through bottle glass, the motions of the old woman who lived up here and the face of others like his friend Joe E., who had worked a portion of the Sandhills land between Wayfare and the river when he was alive. And he heard echoes from the turpentine stills that had rung in the piney woods as the men had labored in order to feed the British navy, dim sounds that spoke of remote seas. It may be that the land we crossed was good only for holding the world together, and that may be why it remained so deso-late that the few lives that had sowed their fates into the pine-shaded sand still seemed to disturb the woods with their commotion.

We took a sharp turn and the truck fishtailed in a patch of deep sand before steadying itself on firmer ground. We had crossed onto land that used to be part of the Murray plantation. It's land that held particular interest for Archie, whose best friend had been Joe E. Murray, until he died. Joe E. and Archie had grown up together, and Joe E. had been Archie's best man when he got married. We passed a break in the pines that gave us a view of a huge pit now filled with muck, water, and weeds. I asked Archie if the Murrays had worked that pit.

"No. That sand pit belonged to another family, a family of mulattoes. Their name was the Smalls. Some of the men in that family, they were real bright Negroes, in color, I mean. And they worked that field there." He pointed to some weeds beyond.

We passed several large gaps in the woods where roads had been cut to provide access to a field. For the next half-mile only a thin and broken line of pines stood as a barrier between the road and the land that Archie called Joe E.'s field.

"That's been in Joe E.'s family a long, long time," Archie said as his hand swept in the general direction of the field. "I don't know the history of how it came to be Murray land. It was handed down to them, I believe. I don't believe it was purchased. Much of the land around here came to the Scots as land grants from George the Third. And the business of giving land grants continued in this area for some time. Back in the nineteenth century a white farmer would build a house, then move a colored family in there. The landowner would give it to him free if he would clear the rest of the land. He would build shacks a good ways apart so the families wouldn't be too close together. And then there were little deals worked out and he'd use them to accomplish his end—go ahead and clear this land up and you can have the land for three years. It was a custom, and a lot of people got ahead that way. There was a good many of them, blacks who owned land. Some of them were pretty industrious, pretty smart. Had to make a living and in the process they'd try something they could make money at. Some of them tried moonshining—probably the only illegal activity that took place up here—way out there in the country, you know. And other than that they'd sell corn.

"And now I do remember when that old woman died," Archie said, showing that he had continued to think about the woman who had lived alone in the woods for so many years. "I remember some of the old patriarchs—those were the old men in Wayfare, the officials—had learned from a hunter that she had died and they went up and got her. They brought her right through town in a wagon pulled by her own horse, I think it was. She was real old, upwards of ninety. She had lived off rabbit, squirrel, deer. There was wild turkey up in there too. She lived long because she was active. A lot of the blacks who were settled in remote places didn't do so well. There were Smiths and others who died young. I don't know, maybe they weren't active enough."

Archie stopped the truck for no apparent reason and let the engine idle. His talk turned to Joe E.

"Melanoma. Started on his back. It started as just a little scratch on his back. But it got bigger and bigger. The scratch on his back got so big that Joe E. went to New York and had a big portion of his back sliced off." Archie talked slowly, quietly now.

"Joe E. farmed this land at one time, but he got out of it. Farmed that field right there for a while. Then he leased his farm and bought himself a pulpwood truck. Found himself a crew, and they started hauling fallen trees off the Fort Bragg reservation and continued to haul wood all winter. I had told him that there could be money in it and so he gave it a try. This was twenty, twenty-five years ago, in the sixties.

"Joe E. was driving old trucks a lot, what with the log hauling and his own rickety old truck, and he said that the vibrations of the truck—that's what he claims—brought it out. Never did get well. He went to doctors all around. Finally they diagnosed it as melanoma. We had a friend, Harold Spencer, who came straight out of medical school and tried to get everybody to stop smoking. You never know what causes cancer. He told me once, Harold did, to quit smoking, but I never would have quit. Down in this part of the country, probably across the entire Sunbelt, it's probably true that sun causes more cancer than tobacco. It would be hard to find a farmer around here who doesn't have some form of cancer. Waynette and I both have had carcinomas and neither of us can stay out in the sunlight. As for other causes, you hardly ever saw Joe E. drink. Thing is, of course, back in those days there weren't liquor stores in Lothian County, or Campbell, for that matter. The only place you could get a drink, you'd have to drive to South Carolina and bring back whiskey. There weren't bars there either, but you could buy scaled whiskey at a liquor store."

I asked Archie what scaled whiskey was.

"You know, whiskey that has been measured for percentage of alcohol. It's got a proof on it, unlike the other whiskey you could buy in those days, whiskey made in places like where we're driving and by people like you and I don't have much to do with every day." Archie laughed and said that homemade liquor could be dangerous sometimes, but so could a sober man. "For fifteen years we've had liquor stores in Lothian County," he continued, "but it's not like some states, like Louisiana where you can get a mixed drink at a drive-up window, or like in Los Angeles where I believe you can buy whiskey in a drugstore.

"Joe E.—after that operation—he got on good for, I believe it must have been three or four years. Then this thing had a recurrence. The doctors suggested he go for surgery, but he decided against it. He decided for chemotherapy and I believe that decision killed him. I went to see him after he had started chemotherapy and it was clear that he had given up. He lost all desire to work. Of course I didn't like to see him when he was in such a bad way, mostly because he didn't want people to come around. I'm not saying I felt good about staying away. And I am not exaggerating here—he had a card table full of drugs in his room. The doctors literally filled him full of drugs. I remember that the colored woman who took care of him would just shake her head when she saw me and say, 'Too many drugs, too many drugs.' After Joe E.'s death his wife moved to Farlanboro. She works with communicable diseases at the hospital. She has a daughter, but I haven't seen that girl since she growed up. After her daddy died my girls and I would take her swimming.

"What's happening to this land is what happens to all land as time goes on. Now there are three people in the current two generations who share whatever profit comes from this land, and as they get married and have kids and die off there'll be more sharers. As you can see, not much is done with it now. I think that the Murrays are having pieces of it logged when they need or want the money. A lot of it, from Joe E.'s field on up to Clay Bank and beyond into the Sandhills, is leased to a hunting club. The hunters and the loggers maintain the road, and the hunters plant corn in the fields to attract deer. There must be two thousand acres in this tract."

As if he were telling a story that had an obvious connection to Joe E., Archie went on. "Talked with a fellow yesterday, Jimmy Jones. He's sixty-five years old. He had his first stroke when he was fifty, but you see he was born into farmland. He went off to World War Two within two or three years of finishing college ROTC. Went into officer training and became the second commander in a tank unit. He saw the Germans one day during a battle and tried to get out of the way of harm. Managed to get his tank turned around, but they hit him with eighty-millimeter fire. At the

Battle of the Bulge it was. Tore the hell out of his back and put him in the hospital for a year."

I wondered if the parallel that Archie was drawing between the stranger's biography and Joe E.'s had to do with injuries to the back. While such a detail might have brought the stranger's story to Archie's mind, it didn't seem the point toward which he was driving.

"Where did you meet this fellow?" I asked.

"It was yesterday, down at the produce stand outside of James Station. I had stopped because I'd seen Jefferson's truck—Jefferson's the one who works that stand—and I wanted to ask him if he was selling any local produce this year. Well, this other fellow, Jones, pulls up looking for watermelons and corn from Florida. After the war he had spent time in England before they shipped him home. Turns out that I had known his brother at State College. In forty-seven or forty-eight Jimmy started buying equipment and mechanized his family farm. He farmed all through the fifties and I believe in the sixties. I used to see him around Wayfare, and it was somewhere during the sixties, before Vietnam started strong, that we had a slack period. Prices were real low: corn was seventy cents a bushel, beans a dollar. But then, hell, it didn't take any money at all back then to make the crop. Tractors cost four thousand dollars then. Oh we'll get back to that—after everyone goes broke with these hundred-thousand-dollar tractors the prices will have to come down.

"Well, Jones decided he'd quit farming in the sixties and became a mail carrier. He had points for the service and the disability from his injury helped him so he got a postal-service job until sixty-five or something and then he retired as a rural mail carrier. He started sharecropping when he was a mail carrier, but it wasn't profitable. Spent all his outside money on farming. Eventually, after he had quit farming, he leased everything. The only equipment he had left was a mower and a one-row tractor. This was twenty years ago. Now he lives in South Carolina. His deal that he was talking about yesterday morning—see everybody's got a different deal—is that he gets one-quarter rent by leasing his land. He can make a little more by farming the land, but what's the point of all the work if he can make nearly as much money by letting someone else do it? He gets one-quarter of the profits and the tenant gets three-quarters profit on corn and beans. On tobacco he gets twenty per-cent of the profits, and he must comply with the program on corn too, and on wheat. That's his deal."

"But what are you saying about him? What does Jones have to do with Joe E. and Murray land?"

"You're looking at the point of what I'm saying anytime you look around you in Lothian County. There's land like this that's used piecemeal and much of it isn't farmed, even though it has excellent soil, because it is not profitable to farm it. There's land that's earning the owners more money by being idle than by being worked. There's plenty of land-owners who make their profit by leasing to farmers who will specialize in a crop, like tobacco, or who earn enough money on the side with another business to keep their farm-ing in the black. To Jimmy Jones I said, 'What did you do last year?' and he said last year he lost money but this year it looks pretty good. So everybody has a deal is the point I'm driving at. At least for the small farmer there is scarcely any direct way to survive just by farming your land."

People, histories, faces, all were slipping into the ellipses that opened up in his thoughts whenever he crossed Joe E.'s land. He punched the gearshift into drive and we continued to wobble through the ruts to the river. "Once, Wayman MacPherson got himself mugged over in San Franciso," he said.

Wayman MacPherson, I knew, lived in the biggest house in Wayfare, a huge white structure with enormous columns and a roof that was now falling in around him.

"After he fouled up out there he came home and laid around for a year or so. Lived with his mother. She tried to run a farm and had a hell of a lot of property. They were the premier family in Wayfare, you might say. Oh, he tried to help her I suppose. She raised cotton. She was a head-strong woman—wouldn't nobody work with her. Wayman, he never did learn anything. But in the navy he broke his left arm and had a concussion—really got screwed up. And then later on he lost his left arm. I don't know what the problem was there, but it was some sort of disease of the arteries, I believe, and the mugging aggravated it. Either that or the mugging somehow caused the problem to begin with. Anyway, his mother—she's the one opened that old furniture store in Wayfare. After she died he inherited it and it became his hangout. He's been all over the world and can tell some stories on hair-raising subjects. His favorite is the campaigns in the South Seas. Those island campaigns—sometimes it would take a day or a week or a month—you never could tell how long it would take to get the Japanese out.

"All the boys in Wayfare used to pick on Wayman be-cause he was comical and, if anything, he became more so after his incident in San Francisco. But he never took a drink after that. At seventy-three or thereabouts he's the only other one of them that age still alive. Will Scott is the oldest of his generation—eighty-two. All the other older boys died in their sixties or seventies. It's a fact that men who move away from Wayfare live longer. For some rea-son men don't live very long in Wayfare. For instance, in my group, of the boys who were around my age and in high school when I was, the three who stayed in Wayfare are all dead. They lived here continuously, never moved, and now they're dead. Of nine or ten that moved away, one, no, two are dead. Don't know if it's food, environment, or what. I guess you can die as well one place as another. Might be boredom."

"Did you move away?" I asked. "You would be an exception."

"Naaw. I can't say that I've ever really moved away. Nothing like the boys who moved to California or New Jersey or Texas. I changed the nature of my relationship to the home place, sure. But you might say I just moved down the road. Farlanboro is just a ways down the road."

Archie kept a cruising speed of twenty-five for the last mile, which was fast considering the roots and ruts. Blackjack oak and longleaf pine closed the road off from the sky. A reddish, tea-colored liquid dripped on the windshield.

"What do you suppose that is?"

"Sap." Archie looked out the side window.

"There's a lot of land, a lot of trees here," I remarked.

"I believe I'd burn it—burn the piss out of it," Archie said and he threw his smoking stub out the window.

/ / / / /

I wanted to stop and go back to Joe E.'s field. The corn that the hunters had planted would provide cover but little food for deer this year. But what else would I find in a field that Archie's best friend had worked before he died? It was a place as familiar to Archie as the faces he passed in his daily orbit, as houses along the route of his nightly walk through the neighborhood that nevertheless continued to surprise him with fresh details rendered supervisible in streetlight: new paint on black shutters, a wing stretching into recesses of a yard. Without such details to yield, this was just a field with stones, bugs, and weeds like any other.

These were just the same old withered leaves of corn. A field is a place where something is always dying. Can a field ever become a trace of the mind and hand that once touched it? Notions of the transformations of death, of the dispersal and unwinding of disintegrated ash and bone, the rising nutrient at the oak's root, the worm in the robin's beak, the berry in the tanager's eye—the field offers these simple consolations to our perplexity. We are all growing into shades around which the feelings of others will accumulate when we are gone. We are all growing into that kind of place where wire grass and lupine grow on ground fit only to hold the world together, a place that comes to be known only as blank space between the highways, mileage markers, and names on a map. Maybe that's why Archie wanted to burn Joe E.'s land.

The El Camino lunged on and in a brief pause between Archie's recollections, I anticipated the river. Much can happen to land that can testify to a person's having lived and worked there. Land can be sold and bought and pass out of mind. It can be divided and subdivided so that the curve of a hill or the thicket of cane a child knew as home assumes the quality of the imaginary. The child who woke up into consciousness of the world there may walk away, may leave his parents and brothers and sisters behind, and return only to view it again during his infrequent visits or as he drives by as a middle-aged man. That story of the land is an old one, one that we all know and tell about our growing up. But a river eludes the buying and selling and subdividing that characterizes the use of land as families and towns grow. The land through which a river flows may change hands, but a river slides through owners' fingers like a garter snake in tall grass. Fences may appear and trees may be cut to block the road to the river's bank, but there will always be other ways to find it. Bridges will always cross it, fences will always be undermined. Something so clean and cold will always run through the heart of a farmer and push its hilarity into the dusty province of his day.

The El Camino lurched over ruts and roots. Archie gently jabbed the stick shift, turned the key, and the truck rolled dead to the bank. His hands performed the ritual: a tap on the pockets, a poke at the ribs for a smoke. He opened the door and stepped out, tossing cigarettes and lighter to the truck seat. He descended the sloping bank slowly, and he walked, his old bucks on his feet, into the river. He didn't reach out to test the water, not that day. He walked until the water, chest high, stained his shirt to the shoulders. He turned to face the bank and fell backwards. Rising, he raked his fingers through his hair, otter slick and tight to his head.

As Archie sat in the river, I walked around the site of the Murrays' old summer cottage. Trees had shaded me from the day's glare until I had entered the circular plot on which the ruined cottage stood. Joe E.'s family had chosen this location and called it Clay Bank because only a hundred yards from the cottage the Lumber River turned, forming a sand and clay bank above what in normal years was a rapidly flowing stretch of current. A sand slope gave easy access to the water, and above the river curve was a broad and deep pool. After the cottage burned down three times, the Murrays left its last incarnation to the elements. Oaks brooded overhead, throwing shadows and light over the broken roof. There was no sound to enliven the empty scene; the river was low and what wind had risen with the heat from the sandy ground failed in the face of the noon sun. Window glass lay scattered on the floor of the cottage, the rugs burned and rotting, the doorjambs doorless. An old couch remained oddly intact, a trysting site for high school students. A tennis court, all markings long since vanished, harbored weeds in the cracks that fanned out over its surface. Nearby was a cooking shelter, its screens torn and limp. Concrete walkways circled the house and extended toward the river. Gathering insects made standing still uncomfortable, and I was ready for a swim. But before I turned away, I saw in one of the partially broken windows a solitary wasp struggling against the corner of a screen for open space. The mood of the place made me sense some esoteric connection between the wasp enmeshed in rows of wire squares, a tractor busy in the folds of furrow lines, and inked figures unwinding in columns on a loan assessment sheet.

The secluded nook in which the cottage decayed stood about ten feet above the river. Although the river was low—lower than Archie had ever seen it—its water flowed rapidly enough to make it difficult to stand above waist deep. The river spanned maybe thirty feet. On the other side grew a tangle of longleaf and loblolly pine, cypress, and turkey oak. Downriver the water lay straight for a half-mile. Twenty yards upriver a large pool opened up, bordered on the left by bays and a bare shore and on the right and beyond where the pool widened out by cypress bearded with Spanish moss.

"Overall, things are drying out," Archie said. "Oh, there are cycles—you have your wet years and then your dry years. But by and large the movement all over the country is toward drying out as people clear more land and remove the trees that trap moisture. There is not as much moisture in the earth here as there used to be. You can see that in the swamp. Now the thing about farming is that dry weather will scare you to death, but wet weather will starve you to death. A farmer recalls the wet years a lot better than the dry years. And I'll tell you why. When it's dry, at least he can move about, check the crop, drive into the fields. He doesn't have the sensation of helplessness at least. A farmer's like tobacco—he'll wait for rain too.

"Of course it depends on how you define drought, as well. Dry weather don't make a drought unless your crop fails. What we're experiencing now could go either way. But if it's going to go the wet way it had better hurry up and do it, or it will be too late. As odd as it may sound, most farmers around here will tell you that we have an ideal climate for what we grow. Most farmers wouldn't change the climate a bit. Dry weather gives texture, flavor, and nicotine to the tobacco leaf. Tobacco likes dry weather 'cause it's a weed. Wet tobacco is no good; it produces a wet leaf."

Archie walked out of the river and pulled a rusted metal chair the size of a love seat from the shore and halfway into the river. He went to fetch a cigarette and lit up, looking like a drenched muskrat blowing steam through its nostrils.

"The question is, what are you going to do about drought? Irrigation is far too expensive unless you have just the right setup and can rig it yourself. Nobody around here will believe in irrigation. There are probably fewer people into irrigation now than twenty-five years ago. The farmers around here who irrigate do it because they picked up the equipment cheap and they have a good source of well water on their land. In California and the desert they have to purchase water by the foot and they run troughs all throughout the fields. Here it's all radial sprinklers. But even with the expense of water out West, irrigation out there makes sense. It don't make a bit of sense where you have a climate that is as unpredictable as ours. In California you can be certain that it won't rain for a month. But here you might could put an inch of water on your crop and the soil will become saturated. But then again it might just rain two inches in the next couple of days and then, boy, you've got problems. What with the soil saturated already and then the extra rain on top of it you could have ruined your crop. So it doesn't pay to irrigate and it doesn't pay not to irrigate. With fifty-fifty odds, and with the memory of years with plenty of moisture, you're not going to find many farmers willing to make the initial investment for an irrigation system.

"Another problem is hail, which will tear up a tobacco crop, makes it look like a field of green rags. I used to carry hail insurance all the time, but it never hailed. Well, one year it did and it paid off. But then, one year after a hail they wouldn't pay off to those who had insurance, and everybody dropped it. They wouldn't approve the damages if you had made your quota for that year. So I stopped fooling with all of it. When they changed the quota from acreage to poundage, the insurance need went out."

So what is drought? A degree of brittleness in an oak leaf? Tobacco that won't ripen? Stunted corn? A certain ratio of evapotranspiration per rainfall unit? When some farmers are crushed under drought and five miles away a windfall rain redeems a field of tobacco from three months of crushing heat, when the farmer would rather have baked mud fields to drive on in order to review a crop reduced to parched sticks than have fields so soggy with moisture that he can't get out there to see what's going on, what can make sense in the farmer's world? Drought becomes any breakdown in the circuitry of work. A flaw in the connection between place and place. An unexpected deterioration of energy, as when, with the release of a photon, an electron drops closer to the nucleus. The sapping of the charge from a system. The world as a dead place, an uninhabited body, a landscape devoid of significance. Nature as the brutal machine. The breakdown of conversation.

Years ago, Archie says, back when he was a boy, they would have a thunderstorm rain every day. "Those were the days of mules and plough boys, before tractors and herbiciders. Everyone would stop working until the storm blew over, and then the hoehands would go back into the field with the mules and ploughs."

Here Archie chuckled as he reminisced. "They were called hoers until the preacher man told them what the word meant and they made the others call them something else. While hoeing out the crabgrass they talked and sang a lot, and that, along with the storms, made for good crops.

"They say that in Brazil and other South American countries they still get rains every day in the summer. That would be near the rain forest, I suppose, or in the Amazon basin. Heat builds up and lifts the moisture out of the forests, and then the storms drop it over the plains. The other day I was watching a documentary on weather in Brazil and Venezuela. During the rainy months, November through March, the Amazon River rises forty feet.

"When Hurricane Hazel leveled Myrtle Beach and the Outer Banks in 1954, we were without power for a week. I was at home, and I don't know why it didn't blow our roof off. But it did get the pack house. As a boy I remember the streams in the swamps were full all summer and in winter the whole swamp was full. Now there's a lot less water. The trend I guess will be to see a shortage of water. They keep cutting timber—they clear land, cut the timber, and there's no place for moisture to gather and generate rain. But then again, it's one thing to be scared, another to starve."

By then I had walked into the river, too, and I leaned against the current as I dug my heels into the gravel. The cold was startling.

"My earliest memory is vivid," Archie said as he sat half-submerged in the river. "Will Scott had a big blue barrel of Buttercup ice cream and he was giving away ice cream from the back of his wagon. In those days, coming along as kids, swimming and ice cream—that said it all. There was a fellow who lived on my daddy's land up above the mill on the pond, Donny Greg. He ran the mill and had two milling days a week, Tuesday and Thursday. Milled corn. I tell you there is nothing like eating hot cornmeal off the mill. In those days there was no real profit for someone milling corn on a small scale. Donny Greg would supply us with meal for the cost of his labor—there wasn't nothing else in it for him. For those two milling days Donny Greg would raise the pond and we could swim in it. In those days the rivers were cleaner than they are now. Of course the Lumber is clean because it's spring fed not far upriver from where we are swimming now. But we used to have to take typhoid shots before school got out in the summer. Kids would swim in ponds with who knows what mess in the water.

"There was a lot more moisture then. Once, during the drought in the thirties, the first big one I remember, I remember asking Sister, one of my aunts, 'Sister, do we always have drought?' She said no, no, it just comes more frequently and lasts longer now.

"And then in 1954 I remember getting out of the service in the summer and expecting to enjoy some good watermelon when I got home. But all there was were thirty acres of sand in my brother's fields. When I got out of the service and came home it seemed like there wasn't much to come home to. The farm was a mess, the family was a mess, and the crops didn't make. Don't know why I came back. Or why I stayed once I did come back. But then, the river was here. At least we had that."

/ / / / /

With our trip to Wayfare and the Lumber River, having come within a city block's distance of the Clare family farm, we had completed the circuit that defined the scope of Archie's daily business. Once we headed home I thought of the ground we had covered that day—seventy-five, one hundred miles—and what we had accomplished. As we drove Archie mused on the way sunlight slants through pines in late afternoon just as it does through venetian blinds. And he talked about the motor on the bulk barn that conked out last year and said that maybe he should check it every night once he barns the tobacco. And he considered the plastic knobs on the dashboard that Beulah, a hunting dog of his, had all but chewed up, and that led him to remember the bird dogs he'd had and lost last year. And he mentioned the time he was in Germany in the fifties when a Swiss fellow invited him and his buddies to visit and they went to see the Alps and to spend all their money. He described the people he'd met out in Colorado skiing. He said drought was referred to in Genesis, where it says that while the earth remains, seed time and harvest, and heat and cold, and summer and winter, and day and night shall not cease. He reviewed the years of wheat, oat, rye, barley, and bean, the kobe, blue lupine, and lespedeza he had harvested in the Sandhills.

He wondered why he didn't get out of farming just last year, in 1985, when he had a buyer for the combine and tractor, when he could have walked away that much less into a debt he would be that much deeper into come September, assuming things continued as they were going or got worse, which they almost always did. He said something about the truck's transmission needing rebuilding, about how the bugs were bad, about how the clouds bumping up against the horizon beyond Wayfare behind us looked like they were on fire, how the whole damn year of weeks had burned up into smoke and scattered like starlings flocking from treetops against the evening sky.

FOUR

"A HAWK with a broken wing—picture it waiting in a cane-brake or briars or sassafras. The hawk would possess its ability to be perfectly still and quiet, and that would help. And then, it would be able to move around quite a bit just by hopping. Its talons and its beak would have remained as deadly as ever. The hawk would have done a lot of waiting, but when a rabbit, a squirrel, or a snake moved in the bird's vicinity, it would have pounced. Otherwise, I don't see how the hawk could have lived."

Archie put his hands on his hips, tilted his head back, and raised his eyes. He was talking about the crippled hawk he'd found one day the winter before down in Bootheel Swamp. He wore thin khakis and a blue short-sleeved oxford shirt with a button-down collar. He wore long pants as he did every day, regardless of how hot it might be.

There had been hardly any softening of the day's heat that Sunday evening in July. Walking with Archie through his neighborhood in the last hour of daylight, I had broken into a sweat before we reached the end of the block. After passing four blocks of houses we took a right on Turnpike, the highway that ran northwest out of Farlanboro. Once we had emerged from under the irregular lines of the old pecan trees that reminded the neighborhood that it had been built on the site of a huge pecan grove, we could finally look up and see the open sky unhindered. Archie had stopped and now looked up at the few stars that shone through the deep blue. Far to the north and west broken clouds appeared as black gaps in the milky blue of the sky, curving beyond the pines on the horizon and suggesting what Archie hardly dared to think: that rain was possible. An occasional flickering of heat lightning flared in the sky. We were enveloped by the hot, humid night air and by the clicking, ratcheting, and buzzing of the cicadas, katydids, grasshoppers, and other insects. Dizzying swirls of gnats and mosquitoes had found us, so we moved on.

"Birds and snakes—they're the same thing, hell. A bird is the snake's future, the airborne thing a snake becomes in a million years. That's what the evolutionists say. Of course the bird will always win." Even in the dark Archie's features appeared sharp, and his eyes seemed more alert than they did in the light of day. The darkness deepened the furrows around his mouth and eyes and blackened the stubble on his face. His eyes had the intensity of an eagle's gaze.

"I first saw the hawk one year, maybe even two years ago. I forgot about it, never thought much about it except when I realized that I hardly ever saw snakes in there. One day last spring Barney was barking like crazy at something and I went up to see what was going on." Barney was Archie's black Labrador, a large, heavy dog that had started hanging around Auntie Jess's house the year before. Archie had begun taking the dog along with him in the truck and finally brought him home to Farlanboro. Archie claims that he knows who raised Barney and that there is little question about the dog's having been abused when he was a pup. I had myself seen Barney cower whenever I picked up a stick for him to fetch.

"Well, Barney had the cripple hawk bayed. Previously, there had always been a lot of snakes down in the swamp on Bootheel Creek. One day when Alec, my son, was a teenager, he wanted to get away from the house so he went squirrel hunting. I told him to be careful of the snakes because he said he was going down into the swamp." Archie chuckled. "He must of shot the gun, it was a little four-ten, half a dozen times. He came out with three snakes and two squirrels. That was over ten years ago, and, well, I haven't seen a snake down there ever since I started clearing and rebuilding that road through the woods. I finally figured out all the snakes that were there had been flushed or eaten by the hawk.

"When I walked over to where the dog had crouched I saw the hawk—it was a red-tail—backed up against a tree. It had enormous wings that he lifted up. But as soon as the hawk looked at me, Barney rushed it. I felt bad that I'd forgotten about that bird, although there's no way I could have kept the dog away. The hawk had been shot, you see, and never healed completely enough to fly again."

Archie slid his hands into his pockets and I heard his keys jingle. "The woods will spook you," he observed. "There are times when there's nothing but birds chattering and you would swear they talk to each other. Like a conversation that drifts around the treetops."

Turnpike cut north out of Farlanboro's residential district through fields of corn and cotton. For much of the year cotton scraps littered the sides of the road. This evening, Archie's dog had followed us through the neighborhood, tracing his own course through yards and garages, then plunging into a cornfield, charging at the sounds and scents of unseen creatures in the corn. Before we turned right off Turnpike to circle back toward the house, we passed an old farmhouse and outbuildings that had been abandoned. The house itself had been neglected and was boarded shut at the windows and doors. Although the fields around it had been maintained and a street lamp near a large cylindrical silo in the midst of the buildings still shed its light in an extravagant gesture, we felt more than saw that the farm was choking in the drought.

Archie had begun to talk about the hawk after I had asked him to explain the system and economics of farming. He had responded after a moment with the story of the red-tailed hawk that couldn't fly as if he were directly addressing the issues of farm economics. Something—a scent in the night air, the sound of Barney racing through a canebrake—something had interrupted Archie and he did not mention the connection between the life and death of the hawk and the farming system.

"It's a hot night. Can't take a walk without working up a sweat," Archie said as he paused to light a cigarette.

"Farm economics are baffling. I'll tell you, you got to get a damn education in it to understand it. And once you get a grip on how to run things and what to do, the government comes in and changes the laws. But okay, it's mostly like this.

"To begin with, the crop reduction—CR—program is administered by the United States Department of Agriculture—USDA—through an agency, the Agricultural Services Commission, or it might be Agricultural Stabilization and Conservation. Either way, it's ASC. We'll look up the correct words on the letterhead, but what it is is the ministry of agricultural policy initiated by Congress. I'm pretty sure that it's the Department of Agricultural Stabilization and Conservation. They're the ones that set the prices your crops will fetch, that issue marketing cards for tobacco, that oversee your allotment, that determine how much land you have to set aside and not put into crops in order to participate in the program, that certify whether or not you're in compliance with the requirements of the program, and so on. The ASC operates at the county, the state, and the federal levels—all of them."

What are marketing cards?" I asked.

"They're cards that you're required to have in order to participate in the program. When you sell your tobacco at the auction they mark the poundage and the price on the cards so that everybody can keep track of which farmers produced how much and so on.

"Now, the financial structure comes from USDA according to what the legislature tells them, and the funds are administered by the Commodity Credit Corporation—it's a corporation but like I say, it's a government corporation. The CCC operates like a bank, and the tobacco farmers' cooperatives, for example, borrow from the CCC the money they use to buy up surplus tobacco. Those loans are paid back, with interest, of course, but only if the surplus can be sold. I think most of the CCC funds come from Congress— I don't see how they could get their own money most years. But then, when they export the surplus, CCC is paid something, either it's paid or—I don't know about that, it's too high up. How the CCC stays afloat making profit some years and losing others, I don't know. That's Washington, D.C., talk that blows around way up there with those birds in the trees."

Archie and I walked east toward the Farlanboro bypass. Cotton fields were all around us now. To our left the railroad tracks crossed the field on an embankment; to our right, between the cotton field and the Lothian County High School, stood the ballpark where community teams played softball. The high school had been built in the midst of what remained of the same pecan grove in which Archie's neighborhood had been built. The school property was bordered by a line of pines that grew alongside a ditch, and large grass fields extended a half-mile beyond the school to the Clares' backyard.

"Anyway," Archie continued, "we're talking tobacco *plus* feed grains, corn, wheat, oats, barley, sugar, cotton, rice, spearmint, butter, honey, cheese, peanuts—we're talking about all agricultural products in this country that are subsidized. If they're subsidized, there's government funds involved, you know. I participate in two main programs. The tobacco program is one, and the food products is the other. Cotton also has its own program, but I don't deal with that.

"I swear I believe that peanuts are out from under crop reduction programs now—and produce never has been in it. In World War Two they needed peanut oil for submarine fuel or something—or in one way or another, it was something they used in submarines—at least that was what they told us. They told you to plant peanuts during World War Two. So then you got market plus on price. They said they used peanut oil on submarines. Now as a cooking oil it produces no smoke—it breaks down to the point that you have no residue. But the part about subs might have been just propaganda—there was a lot of it flowing around in those days."

Archie often leavened his conversation with digressions that usually marked his desire to make abstractions more concrete. The peanut-oil policy had made an impression on him because it seemed so strange when he had heard about it.

"So what are the programs all about? Well, the main thrust is to stabilize the price—agriculture is too quirky a business to succeed without control. It's an inane business is what it is, what with the fluctuations of weather, demand, the prices you have to pay for machinery, fertilizer, and help. A fellow down in Campbell County, Jim West—he's a bit peculiar, a misanthrope you might say, but a good farmer—he showed me a magazine article about farming the other day, and that was the word used to describe farming, 'inane.'

"Now. There are a few main ways to stabilize the prices you receive for your various crops. The most important may be the placing of limits on the amount of product that's grown. That's where the phrase *crop reduction* comes in. In order to participate in the programs you have to leave some land out of production to guarantee that excess surplus won't lower the price. In tobacco it's a matter of having allotments, traditional limits on how much acreage or poundage you can produce. But in the other crops it's a matter of growing as much as the ASC tells you to each year and leaving the rest of your land idle.

"If you're a producer of one of the crops that pays a subsidy, then in order to obtain that subsidy, you must comply. The term is *compliance*. Compliance means you got to plant the allotment on your numbered farm. When you enter farming, or when you become the head of the family operation and you want to participate in a subsidy program, you go down to the ASC county office and apply. When you're accepted into the program, your farm is given a number.

"Remember now, you don't *have* to ever get into the subsidy programs. You can plant what you want and sell whatever you grow on a free market. But the prices you will receive won't amount to what you put into the crop, and so you won't show a profit. That's why the government got into subsidizing farmers.

"Okay, so if you haven't been farming or participating in the program and you do decide you want a subsidy, then you got to plant regular for, I believe, three years. Then you go into the ASC county office and say, 'I need a subsidy.' They'll say, 'Bring us a three-year history,' which means acres planted, yield per acre—all things that you show through receipts—and that all goes to the county committeemen. Then they'll decide if you're eligible. They will try to determine if you are really interested in farming: is your interest fly-by-night, is it to have a family farm, is it for an investment? I believe that their real concern is to prevent the speculation that might come about from people trading farms like commodities. And, of course, it has to do with controlling the amount of crop that's produced by limiting the number of producers at a given time. Sometimes the government will say no, you can't enter the program at this time. Sometimes it won't be left to the county commit-teemen; it will go up the chain of command, up to the state level. But why are you getting the subsidy? Where's the trade-off? The deal is you leave land idle. You are paid a higher price for the crops that you do produce—that's mar-ket price plus the subsidy—because you've agreed to farm dirt, air, nothing. You've agreed to limit the amount of product that you'll grow, that's what it amounts to."

"Does the program simply stabilize the market and pay the subsidy, or does it also buy the crop?" I asked.

"Well," Archie responded, "let's get into that. Let's see." He paused as we approached his yard.

We walked under the pines that marked the boundary between the high school's fields and Archie's yard and pulled up two lounge chairs under his oaks. We sat until the mos-quitoes started biting and then we took our chairs onto the porch at the back of the Clares' house. What the Clares called the porch was an uninsulated, unheated, unair-conditioned room behind the kitchen that Archie had built to serve as a utility room. This back porch was built with bricks—the same bricks, variously shaded toward red or orange, that had been gathered from old tobacco-barn chimneys to compose the exterior of his house. Large win-dows extended from waist level to the ceiling on two sides of the room facing south and west. The windows had both sliding glass and screens and afforded a view of the yard and the trees that divided the yard from the field beyond. A washer and dryer stood against the wall the porch shared with the kitchen, and at the center of the room stood a round cast-iron table with a glass top and two cast-iron chairs, which were rarely, if ever, used. French doors opened onto the dining room, but I had never seen them open. One of the two doors in use opened to the kitchen, the other to the outdoors.

We sat in the thin light on lawn chairs pulled up to the table. One of the very few noticeable sources of tension between Archie and Waynette was their opposing attitudes toward air-conditioning. Even during stretches of the hottest weather, Archie would open up the windows and doors throughout the house. Waynette would protest that his procedure delayed for hours the effective cooling of the house. Archie would complain about the heat, but he always sought the hot, humid air of the porch after dinner. The lights throughout the back of the house were low, the illumination of the porch coming from a curtained window on the door to the kitchen. On the floor and against the wall stood two half-bushel baskets, one full of green and orange tomatoes, the other three-quarters full of butter beans. A row of riper tomatoes lay on the windowsill.

On a small shelf on the wall opposite the kitchen door was a box roughly the size of one that would hold a Monopoly or Scrabble board game, only deeper. The box contained Waynette's stereopticon, a device designed to give three-dimensional perspective to identical photographs mounted side by side on three-by-six cards. The stereopticon was composed of two armatures arranged like a miniature crossbow, with the lenses mounted in a viewing mask and a sliding wooden photograph-card holder that allowed for focusing. Next to the stereopticon was a stack of photograph cards. Archie's left hand held a cigarette and rested on the round glass tabletop as we talked. Lightning bugs, which in cooler summers don't come out in full force until

August, blinked their clear blue-white light, a light so suc-
cinct that they appeared to be stars intermittently covered
and revealed by the oak leaves above. Every few moments
the umber glow of the distant storm silhouetted the trees on
the horizon.

"Okay, now the answer," Archie said. "Here's how the
price thing works. First, the program reduces the amount
of crop that's grown. The idea is to counteract the effects of
having a market flooded with product. The flooded market
keeps the prices low, so low that there is no profit in producing crops to sell at market value. The second main thing
that the programs do is to give you a support price. If
there's a big crop of grain and the market price goes way
down, the government is supposed to pay the difference between what you sell the product for and what they call the
target price. The target price changes every year, but there
are restrictions on how much it can fluctuate from year to
year. It depends on how much product the administrators
figure the country needs. Supply and demand. The CCC issues certificates that represent what you've sold at market
and indicate how far off the prices you received were from
the target price. You receive certificates, then, for all the
controlled crops, and the certificates have a value reflected
by the par price—the farmer's crops can't earn less than
that price—and the granary has to pay you that par value,
which amounts to making up for what you didn't receive
for your crops initially. That's the subsidy—*part* of the
difference between market price and target price. All right
now. That value fluctuates during the negotiable period,
which is not longer than twelve months. The granaries, like
Cargill, will pay you a percentage of the fluctuation from
par up, which last year was as much as sixteen percent.
That is the farmer's subsidy. If I get one thousand dollars in
sales represented by the certificates, I would make an addi-

tional hundred and sixty dollars from the price support. The certificates are nontransferable, and I redeem them at the granary. What makes it work is that *somebody* has got to buy my product if I participate in the program. If markets are slow, then it basically amounts to the government buying your goods.

"I will tell you," Archie said as he shifted in his chair, underscoring his point by gesturing with his right hand in the air, "the economic mechanisms of price support, farmers' cooperatives, allotments, subsidies, parity prices—all of it requires learning a whole new approach. I swear it's just like those farmers that couldn't adapt to mechanization: if you can't figure out what's happening on paper, you're just about finished as a farmer. Even though I know that I don't grasp many of the fine points and that I forget about some of the changes the government makes in the system from year to year, I have just enough of an understanding to where I can get by and do my business. People say that when allotments, crop reduction, and price supports came in in the thirties and forties many farmers were unable to read the documents, certificates, and contracts that the government sent them. A lot of farmers didn't know what the hell was going on. I'll tell you, things now haven't changed all that much, even though many of the farmers these days have college educations. A lot of them won't fool with the federal programs because they don't want to take the time to understand them. Take George, for example, the boy I lease to and work some land with and who helps me out from time to time. He's a damn good farmer and he's damn smart. But he just doesn't trust the programs and so he won't fool with them." It was George's farm we'd stopped at earlier to get Waynette's field peas, the one where the truck was gone. George was a young farmer who traded work with Archie from time to time.

His children had helped Archie barn tobacco, and George had bought several pieces of equipment from Archie. He lived in Campbell County, not far from the Sinclair farm.

Waynette opened the kitchen door, came onto the porch, carefully closing the door behind her, sat down on an iron chair, and placed her cup of coffee on the table. She took off her glasses and rubbed the bridge of her nose. "Don't mind me. You all go on talking. There is fresh coffee made."

Archie said, "That sounds good," hesitated, and then went in to get some. He had been fishing for Waynette to offer to bring him some. When he came back out, I asked him when the government agricultural programs started.

"The federal government's participation in the tobacco business through price support and crop reduction programs really goes back to the thirties. It was a response to the Depression. The New Deal. The feed grains and others didn't have programs until the seventies. As far as tobacco went, the cigarette manufacturers were hardly touched by the Depression, while the farmers were starving. In North Carolina the farmers started agitating when the New Deal was raising factory wages but ignoring the farmers who had been carrying the big companies on their backs. You might say the tobacco farmers were radical and violent back then—they blocked the markets, they organized, they petitioned. Finally they got the government to pressure the tobacco companies to raise the price for the tobacco they were buying. Once the basic elements of allotment, support price, and so on were established, tobacco was a steady earner for your southern farmer until after 1955 or so, as long as demand exceeded supply.

"But then the surplus in tobacco began to pile up. Allotments had been measured according to acre rather than pound, and some of the advances in farming caught up with the system. By 1965 the government had changed from acreage to poundage quotas, but then foreign countries were producing a lot of tobacco, and American tobacco declined in the world market.

"Next thing, a bunch of Republicans led by Jesse Helms decided in the early eighties to give away—to the cigarette manufacturers—the surplus that the farm cooperatives had built up for years. I'll bet they sold the surplus to the companies for a dime to the dollar. With that move the government did precisely what the programs had been designed not to do—they flooded the market with cheap product and that killed prices. If drought doesn't do me in, Helms's tobacco giveaway will.

"Now in a case like tobacco, a government agency watches over the administration of money that tobacco farmers' cooperatives pay in order to support the price. The tobacco cooperatives have to buy up all the tobacco that hasn't sold on the floor of the market, as long as the farmer wants to sell it to them. Right now there's a tremendous surplus and the government is not at this time issuing new allotments. You can grow tobacco without an allotment, but you get no support—so you can't sell it above production cost.

"But when it comes to the grain crops—corn, wheat, and the others—instead of fixed allotments you have compliance, which amounts to doing what they say. When you walk into some ASC office to sign up, to apply for the subsidy, you identify your crops, acreage, and how much you plan to produce. They figure how much you have to plant in order to receive the subsidy. Then you have to plant that amount. The other requirement is that you have to leave idle so many acres for so many acres you plant. If they say to disk it, you disk it. If they say leave it alone, you leave it alone. ASC writes you checks—somebody's got to be responsible for the money, somebody's got to issue the money

—that's what it amounts to. All right now. How do you get your check? You go in—you've been in the business twenty years though it doesn't take that long, you know—you have your history, and you've complied. You have an established yield and allotment and you've left the required amount of land idle. That's compliance. If they say piss on it, then that's what you have to do."

Waynette stood up and said, "Archie, he was asking you about the specifics of your farming, I believe." She went into the kitchen and closed the door.

"These *are* the specifics. In the case of feed grain, say wheat, you go ahead and comply, and then periodically you receive checks. Also the CCC issues a certificate that represents the subsidy that you have coming from the government. It's like a blue stock certificate, only it designates the amount of money that the certificate is worth. How do they know how much it's worth? The ASC figures the worth of your corn or wheat. So you get the market price when you sell the grain, and then you get the certificate made out to you by the CCC. The certificate reflects your yield and the market price received."

"How did you get your tobacco allotment?" I asked. "And how much contact do you actually have with the ASC office?"

"I farm three different tracts. First, there's the tract that Waynette and her brother own; second, a tract that Waynette owns by herself; and third, the acreage up in Wayfare that I inherited. The tracts had traditionally carried a tobacco allotment—not much, but enough for me to farm. A tobacco allotment is just like a tree: it goes with the land. You acquire the land and you acquire the allotment. In my case, where I had a little allotment in Wayfare and others with the other two tracts, I requested the ASC county committee to combine all the allotments. I had all three tracts combined into one farm on paper, so that as far as the ASC is concerned I have one farm and one farm number, even though the land is dispersed. Since I consolidated the tracts into one farm I was able to move the tobacco around from tract to tract. Even though the tracts are in two counties, as far as the ASC is concerned that tract up in Wayfare is a part of Campbell County. Two years ago I purchased additional tobacco poundage from another farmer in Campbell County and I had it put on that same farm number. People are always surprised to see my tobacco appear in a new place where it hasn't grown before, but it's perfectly legal if you go through the channels and get it approved.

"So, I go down to Campbell County's ASC office and I get the paperwork. I participate, like I said, in two programs, tobacco and the grains. I go in to the same office at different times for each program, and I go twice a year for each. First I go in the spring to apply for each program. The programs are run annually. So I go in and tell them what I want to grow and roughly how much I want to plant in all the subsidy crops and they work out the formulas as to how much land I leave idle. Then the second time I go in to the office, in the summer, I tell them the actual acres I did plant in corn, wheat, and what I left idle. Usually that's when I'll designate the tobacco warehouse I'm going to sell at. They will mail the marketing cards a couple of weeks later. Those are the cards you need to have in order to sell your tobacco and receive the support price."

Archie looked at me and opened and raised his hands in a gesture of helplessness that acknowledged that what he had said had fallen short of conveying his best understanding of the farming system.

"Price support is like the food stamp business—in fact, all these programs are comparable. And I still don't see how anybody can make a profit on any of them. I can take the certificate to any granary. Sometimes we don't get these certificates until eighteen months after we've sold the product—I got some coming due this November [1986] for the eighty-five wheat crop. The certificate represents the subsidy, but the value that the certificate represents can be collected in cash or grain. If you don't have any feed grain, if you're a hog farmer or cattle farmer, you can take the certificate and get paid in grain."

He looked at me and pointed to the table. "Now that sounds just fine when you consider it on paper—a subsidy, the government's helping to keep me afloat as a farmer. There seems to be some recognition, just in the fact that we *have* programs, that, when it comes right down to it, what farmers produce is indispensable. But your farmer doesn't get any profit till eighteen months after the conclusion of the season. Last year I was anticipating five thousand dollars and I didn't receive but twelve hundred that year. You see, there's speculation involved in it because you've *got* to comply, which limits your acreage and your yields, but you have no guarantee about what you'll receive for participating in the program because of the fluctuations in the market that occur *after* your growing season. You may not receive even fifty percent of the allocation—that's why so many farmers don't even want to mess with it. And if you start planting without staying in the system—at least every other year—then you lose your allotment. Within one to three years you'll be dropped out of the program. You have a noncomplying farm number."

"Is it hard to get back into the program?" I asked.

"Not really. But it does make for more paperwork, more of a headache—you know. Now, if you went down to the ASC office, like I say, you'd be completely confused. Most farmers simply do what they're told and get their money, like people who never take the time to balance their check-books and just accept the bank's balance."

Intricacies caught him up for a moment before he decided that nuances of his understanding were expendable. He would keep his explanation comparatively simple. He might have been thinking that a specialty in economics is required to manage the crop of paper that the contemporary farmer grows. A muffled roar erupted from the kitchen as the dishwasher entered the noisy phase of its cycle. After a moment the sound of water fell to a low rumble.

"We used to have crop specializations, but now all farmers are growing the same thing. Especially one-man or one-family operations like mine: they'll all farm winter wheat, tobacco, corn, and beans. Unless, of course, they put in cotton or have livestock. It no longer seems to matter how you raise your crop of cash. There isn't enough money in it anymore for farmers to try something new. The only difference between farmers who make lots of money and farmers who make less is the amount of land they farm and where they get their help. And it doesn't matter how much money any of us smaller farmers produce, because by the time it's in our pockets it's owed to somebody else.

"Now George, down in Campbell County, doesn't comply—he plants what he wants. He doesn't *want* to comply. In one of our modern-day versions of sharecropping you can arrange with a fellow to go ahead and plant his crop on your land, land that is already a numbered farm within the system. You tell him, 'You farm my land, comply, earn the subsidy, give the subsidy to me, and I'll let you farm the land at a discount.' I have done this with George some years. George gets the market price for his crop, I get the subsidy. I help George out some, with the discount on the rents, some combine work, and that makes it profitable for him.

"Now this Gramm-Rudman thing required a balanced budget that wouldn't allow the government to owe much money. Well, it connects in there someplace. What the legislation, or the assumption behind it, was supposed to do in 1981, when the price was too high, was to produce cheap exports of beans and corn, to bring their prices in line with the world market. Gramm-Rudman, as far as agriculture is concerned, said, 'We'll reduce the support price, which in turn will bring the market price down. But in order to save the farmer, all you fellows in the agriculture business who sell the farmers fertilizer, insecticide, and seed will have to reduce your prices as well.' Well, so we received the reduction in commodity support and price, but guess what? The reduction of the inputs, fertilizer, and insecticide and the like, didn't come about. The suppliers stuck us. Some of them are charging as much as they ever did. The farmers who are getting out of farming are leaving for that reason."

I asked Archie about a report I had read in a newspaper article that claimed some farmers were receiving more than the $50,000 legal limit in subsidy payments.

"If they are receiving that kind of money in subsidies they have very large farming operations as it is, way beyond the scope of what I do. Everything is tied to supply and demand, even subsidies. It's like with all government programs: some cheat and get caught, some misinterpret the system, more cheat and don't get caught. But the ones that cost the country the most are the ones who do exactly what the government says, those and the banks. Those two, the government and the bank, will lead you straight into debt. Farm debt benefits the bank, but I don't know what it does for the government. When it gets to the point where there's a lot of dissatisfaction, not just among farmers but among people in general, then there are a lot of articles in the magazines on the farming issue, a lot of bullshit on television. But if people are happy, there's no issue. I suppose it's an issue to me because right now I'm in debt. And if I lose my crop this year I'll be in serious debt.

"These young guys still come along all gung ho—they think that they can tear the farming business up. But my attitude has changed. I won't have any regrets if I have to get out of farming. The only regret I'll have is that I won't be able to get what I want out of the equipment, you know, selling it off. I know that for a fact right now. If I do get out and run out of things to do, like cutting that timber on Waynette's land, then I might have some regrets. Then I might become unoccupied, and then boredom may set in and then I may have some regrets. If it ever gets to that point and I've paid off my debts, then I'll probably get back into it in a small way or I'll find another occupation."

Archie stood up and said it was time for bed, but instead of going into the house he punched open the screen door and disappeared outside. As I opened the door to the kitchen I heard him muttering indistinguishable words to Barney, whose tail scraped back and forth on the grass.

FIVE

THE NEXT EVENING we again sat on the back porch in lawn chairs slumped so low that I felt like a small child at the table. At the far boundary of the backyard, three gums and an oak, whose disproportionately large branches stretched over much of the yard, appeared to have been caught in a whirlwind of fireflies as the flashes of a distant storm began to fade. Behind them, the high school's field, large enough to hold a dozen football fields, created the wonderful illusion that we were on the farm. The lights from the baseball park had come on and burned behind a far and obscure line of pines that separated the high school field from the cotton field that lay between it and the railroad tracks. From the house we could hear trains at night, and in the daytime, from the porch, we could see them move, though indistinctly, through the trees.

Just outside the screened door of the porch, on the roof of a small shed that housed the furnace, Daisy, the Clares' white cat, suckled her five kittens. This was about her twelfth litter in five years, the Clares said. The stink that the kittens produced during the hot days permeated the back porch; soon they would have to be moved down onto the ground to take their chances with the dog, the cars, and the toms. Archie said that tomcats would eat the heads off newborn kittens. In that night's moonlight, radiating through a sky still hazy with heat, we could see five blueberry bushes on a strip of grass along the driveway. Next to the bushes sat tomato plants, whose fruit clustered on the vines like walnuts in tight green husks. Barney panted in the yard. Moths fluttered on the windows and the kittens scratched at the screen, pawing bugs. Where the cars and the El Camino sat in the yard, the grass had worn away to expose a patch of dry sand. Like a conversation in another room, the sound of far-off thunder rolling across the sky had occupied the margin of our attention for an hour.

The day had been hot, and Archie had driven alone to the farms that morning. When he returned at lunchtime he told me that we would finish our lesson on farm economics later, after supper.

/////

"Farmers are not disappearing; they're just diversifying. There aren't farmers' wives anymore, for example. The women all work in the new plants, and some of them farm." He had just begun to steer the conversation toward farming when he stood up and walked toward the door into the house.

"Of course, women have always done a lot of farm work around here. My one daughter spent a summer detassling corn, and the other one had a field of watermelons. Much of the help on tobacco and other handwork is still women. There are even some women who are the principal owners and operators of some of the farms. And take George, for example. He farms three days a week and sheetrocks the other four, and his wife works second shift at the new cannery in Campbell County. They both do what they can with the crops whenever they have a chance. The smart ones, the industrious ones, the young farmers—they work two jobs. Small-time family farming is now a part-time business. It's all the result of a rise in technology and employment opportunity. Most of this is a good thing. People should be able to have more variety in their careers and better opportunities. It may be that the only ones you hear complaining about the changes in farming are the old and the tired and the debt ridden, like me. But it's hard to feel good about the small farmer losing out to corporate farming. Corporations can hire lawyers and accountants to do the paperwork, and that makes a big difference."

Archie opened the door to the kitchen and I heard him ask Waynette if she'd seen his glasses. He vanished inside and after a moment returned to the porch with a fistful of papers. He perched his glasses on his nose before turning on the overhead light and sitting down at the table again.

"Now when you sign up for the program to get your subsidy, it says right on the contract that the payment is not guaranteed. You are forced to sign an agreement with flexible terms and figures. That means you must let a certain portion of your land lie idle, you must comply with the program requirements in all other respects, and you still might not receive any compensation. And anyway, there isn't any way in hell you can take back your word not to plant a field when it's too late to plant it. The government gives you a one-way guarantee: you obligate yourself to the government, folks, but don't expect the government to obligate itself to you. Here's what this paper says: 'Notice of Yields and Acreage Bases to All Producers on This Farm. USDA.' This refers to wheat and corn, and here's the order: 'Leave out ten and a half acres.' That's thirty-four bushels times ten and a half acres equals three hundred and fifty-seven bushels.

"Let's say I quit farming myself. I can still maintain the farm's compliance by planting a certain amount, say ten or twelve acres, as long as I meet the requirements. Think about that. The requirements emphasize what you *can't* plant. That makes a whole lot of sense to a farmer. I suppose it's like religion that tells you what you can't do. On the other hand I can lease the farm to someone who will meet the compliance. In that case, the renter won't want the mess of figuring out the program requirements, and the landlord assumes the risk of not getting guaranteed payment anyway. The government money may not come through. So I could go to someone and say, 'Jack, I'll rent this to you at sixty dollars an acre and you mess with the program— get the government subsidy if you comply—or, I'll rent it to you at twenty-five dollars an acre, you'll comply, I'll get the government subsidy, but I'll mess with the government and I'll assume the risk.'

"If you get down to the very fine line of the instructions —they're not laws, you see, you could call them regulations—many who do it this way would not be operating according to ASC regulations because the payment is supposed to go to the *producer*. It's the producer, the one who actually grows the crops, who is supposed to comply and who is supposed to receive the payment.

"What I've done with George some years is I've found in him a producer who doesn't want to comply and only wants to lease. Now some of the land I'm leasing is Waynette's family's land and I don't *personally* own it, and her brother insists on getting the subsidy payment. So if I farm the land I get twenty-five acres free rent and what comes off the land. 'You reap the wheat and I'll reap the payment'— that's about what he's saying. Now let's say I don't want to farm it, but I want to rent it—which is something I could do just because I usually farm it, I control it, and I've always dealt with all the ASC mechanisms. The fellow I lease it to could go down to the ASC office and say, 'I'm the producer. I should get the payment.' But the ASC would just tell him, 'All right, son, go work it out best you can.' Up in Washington they don't care about the trading.

"If someone comes up to me and says, 'Do you get a subsidy?' I can honestly say yes. But if they ask, 'How much do you get?' the conversation could go on forever because I don't know that I get *anything* out of it. It's just business. Any farmer would know what you're talking about. Right on the Wheat and Feed Worksheet it says, 'All benefits are subject to reduction in accordance with the Gramm-Rudman-Hollings Act.' In May I was supposed to receive five thousand dollars, but I got twelve hundred in the form of a certificate of payment. I'm supposed to receive another in October, but I still haven't seen all the money for last year's and this year's compliance, even though I have got some of the certificates."

Archie removed his glasses, set them on the table, and pulled himself upright in his chair. As he paused, one of the kittens leapt up against the screen and batted a moth. I thought back to early that morning. One of Waynette's friends had driven over in her royal-blue Skylark to pick Waynette up to go shopping. When the woman started the engine, she and Waynette heard a dull thud from under the hood of the car. It was common during the winter for kittens and cats to crawl up under the hood into warm places inaccessible to dogs, and one of the best spots seemed to be between the blades of the fan. As I had stood in the kitchen, Waynette came in and asked if I would mind taking care of the kitten that had just been killed by the fan in her friend's car. What had led a kitten to crawl up into the hot engine in July remained unclear. Archie had already left. I could see in Waynette's manner that she had witnessed many kittens' deaths. Unable to find a shovel, I took Archie's maul and headed out a few dozen yards beyond the oak and gums. The grass was still dewy and the sandy soil was soft where I broke the ground with the maul blade. I dug little more than a divot in the field, a foot or so deep, and when I placed the white kitten in the soil its body was still warm.

"Okay. If you want to know what the farmer's up against, here it is." Archie, after a lull in his speech, had found what he considered to be a good story that would illustrate the condition of the small-time farmer.

"I had to take the combine down to South Carolina for some work about a month and a half ago. That's about a fifty-mile round-trip—a long way for a combine. I took it down there to have it cleaned, and while I was down there I told them I thought I had an oil leak. It appeared to be a bearing, a crankshaft bearing. I said to clean it up, fix the bearing, and repair the oil line so I'll know what my oil pressure is. I called back down there and the shop man says I didn't have a bad bearing, just a leak in the block from the screw where the line inserts into the motor. A screw had just loosened up and the fan blew it around, nothing to it. So I said, well, that ain't much. That's good news.

"When I went back down there they had a bill for five hundred bucks. I was already out the gas and the time to get it down to South Carolina. All that just for a screw!

"What the shop had done, they'd looked for things to do. They replaced a chain, two belts, and so on. They fixed the steps to the cab, steps that had been bent for ten years. They went and straightened them out. In other words, they fixed unnecessary things. All I can do is say I didn't ask them to do all that work, but the thing is, the work had been *done*. I ain't got an argument. Ten years. And the man that wrote the bill wasn't in the shop. I don't know what they figured. The thing is, I haven't paid and I'm not going to break my neck to pay. I take the combine down to South Carolina at seventeen miles an hour, I take the header off it, and now I'm the worse off for the trip. That's the story of the farmer. Your farm is just a place where banks put some money and these other fellows come along to take whatever they can of it."

"You talk a lot about the price of inputs, the materials required to grow a crop, being too high. Is that what keeps the price of the commodities high?"

"As I understand it, the part of the Gramm-Rudman law dealing with agriculture was devised to put a reduction in the production and in price support of beans, corn, tobacco, all of them, I guess. They were at the point where the export price had gotten too high and foreign countries weren't buying them readily. The Common Market responded to worldwide scarcity by producing enough grains to stop importing and to begin exporting. So many of the world markets have just about dried up. Once a crop surplus has built up it is inevitable that prices will fall. Our government was trying to cut the prices down so that American crops could compete in the market again for export. The first year the USDA cut corn a dollar a bushel, but they didn't cut the inputs, so that year they cut my income nine thousand dollars *in corn alone.* In wheat the price was cut from about three-fifty to two dollars—you had a bigger cut in wheat than anything else. Tobacco went from about one dollar and eighty-three cents to one-fifty, about twenty cents, due to the support being cut."

Archie sat forward in his chair and reached for his wallet in his back pocket. He opened it up and began a methodical search of its contents as he talked.

"Like I started to say a while ago, we get no subsidies on tobacco. Tobacco farmers only get a support that comes from what they put in it themselves. It's like we tax ourselves to support the price, and that is managed by the tobacco growers' cooperatives. And the price follows support. So wheat, corn, and tobacco came down; soy dropped from 1984 to 1985, say a reduction of one dollar a bushel that year. All that means thousands of dollars to me. It means cutting out all the profit. We're expecting about six dollars on beans this year. Until now beans have been in the neighborhood of eight-fifty."

Archie apparently had not found what he had been looking for, so he refolded his wallet and put it back in his pocket.

"A reduction in inputs—seed, fertilizer, insecticide—has started this year, but it's the result of years of massive profits these companies have garnered, and they still aren't losing a bit of their profits because the farming is more intensive. The big corporation farms must be using more chemicals per acre in order to achieve better yields. And then, too, the small farmers are starting to learn that some years they can get by without putting as much fertilizer, herbicide, and pesticide on the crop as they normally might. The small-time farmer is making these decisions because he has to cut back someplace in order to turn a profit or just break even. The chemical companies are realizing that they have to hook small-time farmers back into the system to keep them dependent. Even though there's a slight reduction in the cost of inputs, it's nothing like the reduction in price support or the reduction in the price of the product that the farmer receives. The companies have always said that they didn't need to lower the price of inputs because better yields year after year would give the farmers their profits. It takes about a dollar per acre to produce wheat, and this stays pretty constant. But consider: even if the inputs have a twenty-percent reduction, we get a fifty-percent reduction in the prices we're getting on the market, and how are you going to make up for that with better yields per acre? So debt is *built into* the farming business."

He said "built into" with an emphasis that identified this designed contradiction as the greatest folly imaginable. Archie cleared his throat and rubbed his hands on his cheeks as if to feel whether or not he needed a shave.

"And, of course, we're overlooking the initial cost of machinery. Unless you inherit machinery, you start off farming in debt. Take the combine. It will do a lot of work for you, there's no denying that. A combine separates the wheat kernel from the chaff. But in oats and barley it won't separate. It will separate the seed, but the process is more complicated. Rice, barley, and oats each have to be milled differently. A combine gets wheat to where it's ready to be ground, but the others have to get through another process to get ready to be ground into product. For the combine you're talking about a cash outlay of thirteen thousand dollars the first year, what with the down payment and your monthly. You've put in over twenty-five thousand dollars by the end of the second year you've had it, and you haven't begun to buy the thing yet. Now we're talking about the cheapest one new, the smallest, which costs thirty-five to forty thousand. You're talking about a machine that would *never* be paid for on the scale of farming I do. You'd need about five hundred acres of wheat, five hundred acres of corn, and five hundred acres of soy just to make the yearly payment.

"It all moves to favor the big farmer," he continued. He propped his elbow on the table and closed his hand into a fist. As he talked he rubbed his thumb against the side of his index finger.

"The family farm used to make it off of tobacco or hogs. There were ways to do it. Run corn through hogs and you make twice the money. If you sold the thirty-five or forty bushels of corn that it takes to make two hundred and twenty pounds of hog, at three dollars a bushel you wouldn't come out ahead anyway. But when the price of corn drops to one-fifty a bushel, and pork stays the same price, the pork producer is going to make money. But if you're going to raise livestock in the South, you better be around them, live right there, I mean. If you're off the place, first thing you know you'll lose a cow, and then the same with hogs. You've got rustling in these parts. My brother John lost a truckload of cows that were kept on land up in the Sandhills, and he lost them simply because nobody was living there. Forty-five or fifty cows. He never figured out who stole them. That's what you're running into if you can't watch them yourself. You'll either lose them through just plain thievery, or through sickness. I did it one year. I had my own cows and fattened them up. I made a little money, but I didn't make enough to justify having to drive down there at least once a day. I tried it and saw that it wasn't going to fit in, so I didn't go ahead with it."

Waynette came out onto the porch, announced that it was ten o'clock, and told Archie not to leave the stereopticon and photograph cards out where the humidity would ruin them. Archie had brought the box down from the attic for me to see. He reached over for the box and handed it to me. I looked through the thick lenses at a picture of Niagara Falls and then at a picture of workers in a field of cotton.

"This must remind you of your air force days in Germany when you spent your time looking through a stereoscope at the landscape of Europe," I said.

"I suppose, yeah, there's a similarity. But this thing is just a toy."

I had seen the stereopticon cards in antique stores before and never understood why the two identical pictures were mounted side by side. As I looked through the thick lenses I was reminded of the stereoscopes I had as a kid and of the disks that rotated to show three-dimensional photographs of Zorro and Fury.

"That device will give you a good idea of what it's like to try to see the farming business on paper. You look at the photographs themselves and there's nothing to 'em. You think, That's no big deal, that isn't as impressive as being there, there's a place just down the road on my own street where the beech tree and the view of the sunset are more than any one of these pictures can match. The flat picture is just a scrawny thing. Then you view it through the stereopticon and it's kind of neat again. Some of the grit, some of the wonder is put back. Of course what you're seeing, and the sense it gives you that what you see is real, is an illusion. Sure it's interesting with depth added. But it's an interest that's alien to the business of working in the world that the photograph tries and fails to capture. So our talk tries to make a more interesting picture of farming than the news reports, the contracts, and the other farming papers can, even if the picture isn't very pretty always. What our talk can never capture—I'll tell you what that is, buddy, that's time. That's walking through it all, through the fields and groves and barns and lifting them all up and hauling the world on your back through the days, weeks, and years and seeing a crop grow up and seeing it slip through your fingers. That's the element of time. It all flows through time."

Although I wasn't quite sure exactly what Archie meant to tell me about time, I did see that in talking about the details of farm economics it would be all too easy to lose focus. All of the policies and papers were designed to govern and to respond to the actions and produce of real people in the real world. But I only half understood Archie's metaphor of the stereopticon.

The hour was late, and a hint of cool air brushed through the screen, carrying the scent of damp grass from the field. I wanted to fight off the inclination to go to bed so that I could prolong that delicious sensation of autumn that arises and collapses within a few rare moments on some summer nights. It is almost as if at those times we could sense the planet wheeling in its orbit, as if the inevitability of the drought's passing had become palpable.

Sensing my puzzlement over his stereopticon metaphor, Archie seemed to want to try again. He bent over the table searching through his papers until he selected one and laid it on top of the others. "If you want to understand the farmer's problem, look here." He stubbed his forefinger against the paper. "Here is the snake in paradise: here's something that isn't at all what it appears to be. This is the loan assessment. Even though I'm in debt, the bank will give me anything I want. Hell, the bank *encourages* me to take what I want. You can look at your assets all you want, and there ain't a bit of profit to be found. But the banks count the property, which I can't sell. Nobody would buy it. I've tried. They count your machinery and buildings, even though they aren't worth anything to anybody but me. They count the house, and my tractor and truck, and Waynette's car, but hell, who's going to put those things on the line? The problem is, you look at this loan sheet and it says I'm doing great. But not a damn bit of what they count produces anything we can live on, let alone pay the debt with. The truth is nobody really owns anything; you just can't own anything these days. Don't know if you ever could."

His voice had risen with an earnestness and bitterness that caught him up for a few moments. He had allowed himself to become exasperated. He sat back down and lit a cigarette and said, as if to himself, "That piece of paper is what farming has amounted to—farming has become something a farmer can scarcely recognize.

"I had the machinery paid off, but then I had to use it for security on drought loans. In the drought of 1978 I used government help money. Not free money. That first loan in seventy-eight was at three percent interest, in eighty it was four and a half percent, and the third one was nine and a half percent. No one took it the last year. So the machinery and the land are collateral. My debt is from the seventy-eight and eighty droughts. In seventy-eight we had a return of about zero. We had to borrow thirty-five thousand dollars to pay off the input debt. In eighty I had a return of about twenty-five percent of what I normally got. But of course it wasn't enough. And then you borrow to pay off for that year, for all the inputs you need in order to make a crop. That's where farming had gotten so expensive that one year can break you. But I was handling that debt okay until eighty-five. We were in good shape until prices started tumbling. We did all right in eighty-one, eighty-two, eighty-three."

Archie picked up the stereopticon cards and flipped through them. He took his glasses off and rubbed his eyes.

"That's the big problem with farming in this country. It's not profitable enough a business to withstand disaster. You used to could do it, but you can't anymore. My daddy educated his children on an income from a small tobacco farm using day labor, hand labor, and mules. With technology all your labor is gone. Then it was three dollars a day, now it would be thirty dollars. But then we grew up hunting fox in the woods, and now kids chase cartoons on a computer screen. According to that loan assessment, I'm a good investment. They would love to see me go on and get loans every year until the bank walks in here and takes the title to the house and land. Do they think *they* could sell that land, I wonder?"

He stood up, walked over to the screen door, and looked out. I could hear Barney panting as he crawled to a stand and then sat, waiting for Archie to emerge. "Got to look at that corn in the morning," Archie said. For the last couple of weeks those words had become an evening refrain. Since drought had frozen him in inactivity, he had poured the energy of his imagination into the sweet-corn patch. I believe that when Archie reminded himself to check the sweet corn on a hot night in the drought of eighty-six , he was thinking about the other crops that surrounded his corn patch. I believe that when he spoke of checking the corn he was thinking about the circuit of land and activity that he had drawn around his life, about living away from the farm, about the things he had done and not done. The sweet corn wouldn't make him any money, but it would allow him to bring a full bushel from the farm. Everything else was waiting like sheep in the meadow—debt, drought, July's promised departure, August with its foot in the door—but the corn. When anyone asked, What's on for tomorrow? and when nothing else would do, there was still sweet corn. "Got to look at that corn in the morning."

We went into the kitchen, expecting to call it a night. Archie carried the stereopticon box in one hand and his bunch of papers in the other. The phone rang, and Archie set what he was holding on the table and answered the phone. It was Auntie Jess down at the Sinclair farm. Archie hung up and grabbed his hat. "Come on, let's take a ride. They say they see someone burning a fire. It's probably nothing. They're scared to go out at night and won't go look at it." I climbed into the truck. Archie let Barney ride in the front with us.

As we turned from the driveway onto the street, I saw Waynette through the picture window as she sat down in the living room with a book in her hand. Waynette's income from the country high school must have provided a great deal of security to the family. Her salary alone would have supported just about any of the households in Farlanboro. Yet Archie seldom mentioned that her salary had kept them afloat during the last few unproductive years. In comparison with her steady income he must have felt that what he made on the farm was marginal. Because his income was unstable and every year the decision to invest in the production of a crop was a gamble, he may well have felt that his farming had become less an occupation and more a pastime.

"When I was in school I took a course. Didn't think much of it at the time. Economics. And what it dealt with was things like distribution of property, things the government could do to ward off a depression, world trade, things like that. The teacher's attitude was positive. 'There will never be another depression,' he said. So far it has worked, cash flow and all. You have a widespread economic collapse when there's no money in circulation. There were things the government had done—the pork barrel thing—by pumping money into agriculture. They could stimulate rural economics, and back before World War Two practically everything was rural. For a long time the big push had been to industrialize the South. Get away from agriculture. Get manufacturers into North Carolina. Well, we've learned about the efforts to industrialize in the fifties and since, now that they've been successful to a degree."

A car that had been tailgating us roared as its driver gunned the engine. Archie made no comment about the unintelligible words the people in the car shouted as they sped by. As I turned to look at the passing car I saw Archie in profile, staring forward as if oblivious. Barney also stared ahead, his mouth open and panting.

"There's still a good living to be made at farming, and maybe in part it's because so many rural people can work in manufacturing now, what with the new factories and plants. That economics teacher said that there will always be times when those who have lots of property, unless they're on their toes and have other means, will lose it—through bankruptcy and inheritance, sold for money or divided among children, cut up into small tracts. Unless you're very careful at these periods of low prices, you'll have to sell your property. All this stuff is not new to me. It was not new to me when I heard it in college, and I haven't forgotten it now. Eventually, it seems to me, the balloon will bust and we'll have another depression."

The warm night air swirled about in the truck cab. Far to the south we could see beams from searchlights wandering around the sky. Archie said that they were in South Carolina.

"I had a friend, Old Man Maxton," he began again, "who had no formal education. He was a dirt farmer, but he had family money. A couple of years ago he built himself a hundred-and-fifty-thousand-dollar house. I asked him one day how in the hell he was going to pay for that. Well, he was the type who had a bunch of money and equipment handed to him. He inherited a cotton picker, three or four tractors, bulk barns—everything paid for. He had no payments except on the inputs for any given year. His farm was a damn machine handed right to him. All he had to do was crank it up. He had never had to really work for what he had, and he continued to feel insecure about it. He'd say, 'Buddy, one day it'll blow up!' He just farmed his land and made a profit because all his equipment was free and clear. But he still thought it was only a matter of time before all of his possessions would be worthless. He was scared to put any money into his farm. I guess he's an example of a rich man who makes himself feel good by adopting an attitude that says make just enough to get by and don't ask for very much or you'll be disappointed. A rich man who pretends he's poor. Maybe he was right. He's dead now." Archie raised his right hand as if to say, what can you do? "But he was right that it's best to be conservative in farming.

"The odd thing is that every one of us is sitting here waiting till things get better. The young ones especially. All young farmers are enthusiastic. They continue to get new equipment because they can make the payments. They're young, that's the main thing. They can go ten to fifteen hours a day. Some of them are good managers, and some of them have been left some good equipment."

Archie seemed to admire the young farmers so much that I began to wonder if, given a second chance with youth, he wouldn't do it all again exactly the same way. Despite all the drawbacks involved, farming had retained its attractiveness for Archie.

"The way you got to do it today is like George. George and his brother sheetrock one week in Raleigh, one in Atlanta, the next in Charlotte. And also, George's brother's in on the crop. Which was a damn smart thing for George to do, see. Because the brother runs the contracting business and he wants George to work with him. They leave late Sunday night and come back on Thursday. But because he's in on the crop with George he'll make sure that George has enough time to work it, and he'll help him, too. I just about had my grain bin sold to George. Now the thing about George is, if he makes money, he's going to spend it on farm equipment. He's got a thirteen-year-old daughter and they're going strong, you know—they live to work. Takes a special breed to do that. They got a son, he has a wife—she's a good girl. She's an Indian, kind of shy. She was a Locklear. Locklear's actually an English name. All of them are English names now."

/////

I was surprised at how few house lights we passed on the highway. Even though I had driven this route many times before, I had never realized how desolate it was, how long the stretches between houses were.

"That's a good old boy working that place." He pointed to a garage on the side of the highway.

"Got his six-year-old boy working with him—he's screwing screws. You see it doesn't matter that he really do anything except cultivate the habit of working. I gave him a lecture one day. I said stick with your dad and you won't ever have to go to school. That got his interest.

"Another aspect of farming in this part of the country is what takes place between people and the work they do, not just the papers they exchange. True sharecropping under the old system meant that the farmer would furnish the land and the fertilizer—that's if it was fifty-fifty sharecropping—and that's about all. The tenant would live free of rent and do all the labor. If the tenant had mules, he'd work it with mules. If the tenant had a tractor, he'd work it with a tractor. At the end of the year the owner and the tenant would settle up and each one of them, the laborer and the owner, would receive half. There were other arrangements, too. All the variations had to do with how much the owner put into the crop and how much the tenant would receive. If the owner broke the ground or worked the crop in any way he'd get a larger percentage of the profit.

"Now that system no longer applies. It's done for. You don't see many tenant houses anymore—all that's changed now. If you're getting into modern-day sharecropping—I did some of that, from the tenant's end. I performed the labor and provided the equipment."

The dog's head moved between us so Archie talked around it. He fiddled with the gearshift to make sure that he wasn't in second gear. The air was sharp with cigarette smoke.

"A local woman—her husband's dead—furnished the land, fertilizer, and seed. I did everything else. She received half of the profit and I received half. Now the point is that you try to make it so that the investment is equal to both. So that neither has the advantage over the other."

We turned into the driveway at the farm. The wooden stand, where Dan L. had said he would sell produce that year, was empty. He hadn't posted any signs yet, and it was clear that this fueled Archie's skepticism about the prospects of Dan L.'s actually following through with his plans. We didn't get out of the truck, but drove underneath the willow oak and paused in front of the porch. Archie looked past me and through my open window to the front porch, where Auntie Jess slowly poked her head out the door and motioned past the grain bin toward the pond.

"Where's Jeeter?" he asked. Auntie Jess shook her head as if saying no and looked down. Dan L. appeared at the front door and asked Archie to come up and sit on the porch awhile. Archie said he didn't have time, waved, and drove off.

We approached the edge of a field bordered by a row of pines. "Planted those pines twenty-eight years ago." We could see flames through the trees, two spots of flickering light that, when we approached, separated into a small fire on the far shore and its reflection on the pond. We slowed to a stop and Archie turned off the ignition with the transmission still in drive.

"Just someone fishing, using the fire to attract fish. Auntie Jess, Dan L., they won't look into things at night, or at least that's what they've led me to believe. They may be superstitious. But there are probably other reasons why they called us down here tonight. The man who used to live in their house was a colored preacher and everyone knew and liked him. He was accepted here because he was a preacher, and because he'd lived here forever. But the area has become an Indian area, and the Indians don't like the blacks living here."

Archie started the engine, turned the truck around, and headed toward the house.

"Now the reason we're here might be something else. It might be that Jeeter was getting out of hand, or maybe it was Dan L. himself. Auntie Jess may have thought Jeeter was going to steal the truck, you never know. Something along those lines most likely.

"The old ones want you to come around, shoot the shit. Don't even amount to nothing. That's the way the old ones are. She's worried about Jeeter, who's about the age that he'll run off. There isn't anything for him to do. He's of that age." He sighed. "You remember last week she was raising hell about me not giving him work. I told her, 'Hell, Auntie Jess, there isn't going to be a crop to work this year. And what's more, the way the business is these days, I got to quit farming—I told you that. I ain't got any work for your boy.' Whatever is going on tonight may be just part of things changing."

Archie drove south on the highway down to Johnson's Grocery, which was closed for the night. Archie seemed to have a line of credit at Johnson's, and we stopped there almost every time we passed. He rarely paid cash, but no questions were ever asked. A sign near the gas pumps read "Tough Tires With Tougher Warranties." Near a pay phone others read "Pepsi," "Winston," and "Good Gulf." Archie pulled into the lot and turned the truck around. It was at Johnson's Grocery that he had found the tractor after it had been stolen the year before, and it was at Johnson's that Jeeter made the telephone calls he didn't want his family to overhear.

"I'll tell you something. An Indian won't ask you for a damn thing, and if he does he'll pay you back. The young

Indians won't ask you for much—they've got some pride. Used to be you had to appease 'em to get 'em to work. The main thing with me in relation to Indians at the farm—it is strictly business. They want theirs right down to the penny if they're in the field. The trick is that you got to give them what they want. If you haven't paid them, maybe one or two won't show up. So I pay them what they want 'cause if you don't they'll leave you with a crop of tobacco in the field, and no way one man can barn a crop of tobacco. No way.

"But Auntie Jess's something else. I can tell she's getting around to asking for money. There's sharecropping for you; she'll always find something to ask you for. She just hasn't had the nerve yet—that's the way she is. And then, you were there the other day and she wouldn't bring it up with you around.

"We're in about the same situation, if you look at it that way, Dan L.'s family and me. We're both dependent on the government and it's not doing either one of us any good."

We didn't see Jeeter or anyone else at Johnson's. After we sat in the parking lot for a moment Archie shifted into gear and pulled onto the highway. Heading north back to Farlanboro, we could see a distant glow in the thick night air. That would be the town itself. Archie had mercifully put Barney in the truck bed. The trees of Bootheel Swamp closed in around us and the insects filled the night with a sound like rushing water.

"Getting back to the big picture. It will take at least five years to reduce the surplus of the flue-cured tobacco cooperatives in this country. The government, they aren't going to tell you anything about the price until a week before selling. When the Democrats were up there everything was open, aboveboard. You'd know what was going on before you planted. Like it is now, everything is secretive. You've got nothing to plan with. It adds just that little bit more to the stress of farming. At my age that bit more plays a damn important part. If I was young it would be full speed ahead, who gives a damn! I worked during the Nixon administration. Nixon had it all over Reagan as far as the farm front is concerned. Reagan—someone has him all wound up over military arms we don't need. Nixon had sense enough to know that the country came first. Reagan doesn't have that patriotism. Farmers can get what they want out of the Democrats, but then so can everyone else. On the whole, Ronald Reagan will go down as a good president 'cause he slowed things down. As far as working under him as a farmer, it's hell, boy. No, you can't blame it on a single party. Well, if you're politically minded you're going to blame it on one party or the other. But that ain't the way it is."

The pointless drive to the farm, the secrecy of Auntie Jess and Dan L., the uncertainty about what was really going on that night had all combined with Archie's fatigue to put an edge on his words. He would have said that he was "riled up."

"It's surplus. Can't get rid of the forces that lower prices and build up surplus. It's worldwide economics, our own government's economic policies; it's changes in the world market. The Reagan administration is so damn secretive it drives me crazy. Jimmy Carter ain't never been anything but a con man. Didn't like his personality—he didn't have any sense. He wasn't a politician. Didn't do shit. He was scared to death. Well, Ford didn't do shit either. Carter knew damn well he didn't need to do a damn thing. The country was ready to try something else after Ford. Being faithful to a party is a bunch of bullshit. But I'll say one thing. When it comes right down to it, whether you consider the politics, economics, the loan office, or the crop, farming is just a mess of paper. That's where it's been headed, and that's where it has ended up."

I could hear in his voice a calm determination to find rest from his worries, rest from another day of drought.

"I'll tell you what. The mess of papers on my desk at home right this minute adds up to one thing: if I lose the crop this year, I'm through with farming. That's the truth.

"Look out there in that swamp. Can't see a blooming thing. There are snakes in those woods. You may not see them, but they're there."

/ / / / / / /

SIX

FIRST THERE'S a hoarse crow, a sputtering blue jay, the murmuring undermoan of mourning doves, a cricket's whistle, the ratchet of enduring cicadas. Half an hour later it's the rumble of a train that seems to split the house in two, and then, with the return of gray light, the low thunder of guns from Fort Bragg. And then comes a sensation that says the morning must be cool, that all the doors and windows in the house must be open. The air conditioner's envelope of sound is absent, and the humid air presents the facts of this Saturday morning in the third week of July: in the backyard the El Camino sits under the low branch of the oak, a ribbon of red ants unreels at the edge of a bedsheet on the clothesline, Archie has already been to wherever he goes and returns from this time of day and now sits in one of the lawn chairs near the El Camino in a cloud of gnats and smoke.

Morning usually rattles and scrapes its arrival. Somehow my sleep has survived the first call of day: the sound of stainless steel on porcelain, the ring that finds amplification in wood paneling and sheetrock, finally reverberating in the very rafters, grafting along each pipe that lends its skinny bone to the skeleton of the house, residing, abiding, swelling somewhere between the tympani of ears and the tensed roots of teeth. So the world calls, usually. The doing of the dishes is always like that.

But the timing of that act of imposing order appears in the Clare household as a fundamental rite of civilization.

The old idea, preserved by stale texts from sixth grade geography classes, is that saving rather than throwing away the dishes marked the inclination of our prehistoric ancestors to settle down, to build a life, to shift the archaeology of culture from the ash heap to the brain, to take out a second mortgage. And the supreme modern extension of that civilizing act is the harnessing of the river, bringing the millrace into the home, damming the current with the valve in the tap. Maybe the clatter of dishes has more to do than we suspect with the racket of insects in willows and oaks, with the flutter and scare of a covey, with the slap of a wood duck's wings on water. There is still something of the rush of whitewater in the cylindrical stream that issues from the faucet, something of the foam and wrack of eddies and twigs in the sediment of the drain screen. The Clares bracket their day with this return to the river, even though it is achieved by bringing the river to themselves. No, they do not feel the sand between their toes or bend to slap the yellowflies from their calves, but they can smell the trees in the tap water. And the dishes—they ring out with all the clamor of the high life.

The front half of the brick house they built holds the living and dining rooms, painted a pale aqua green that magnifies light and banishes shadow. Both rooms are still, formal, almost radiant in their austerity. A hall leads from the foyer inside the front door to the three bedrooms. The back half of the house forms one long room. The kitchen work area is at the end near the back porch, an informal dining area next to it. Against the far wall are a desk and bookshelves reaching to the ceiling. The entire room is walled with dark knotty pine, including all the cabinets. A large mantelpiece sits above the brick hearth in the wall that divides the two halves of the house. Centered above the mantelpiece is a framed Audubon print of a wild turkey.

To its left hangs a tobacco "hand"—a gathering of twenty or so tobacco leaves wrapped together at the top end with another leaf. A small circular rack holds Archie's father's pipes. Next to the pipes sits a small rectangular tin that held his seed for one season's tobacco crop. On one of the top shelves of the bookcase stand two framed aerial photographs of the Clare family farms in Wayfare. The one on the right shows Archie's parents' house and the surrounding foliage of magnolia and holly and the silver-brown branches of leafless crepe myrtles. Across the top of the picture stretches the pale sky blue image of the large millpond on the Clare land, spattered with cypress trees and rotten cypress stumps near the shore. The photograph to the left shows the house Archie's grandfather built, where Archie's spinster aunts lived, the house that has since been expanded to accommodate the larger family of a younger generation. A willowy stand of pine blurs the left margin, and the blue water of the millpond borders the top. Together the pictures do not give a continuous view of the property, but one can easily imagine the lay of the land that stretches between the two houses.

On the wall above the kitchen table is a framed poster. Two boys, two or three years old, wearing T-shirts and overalls, stand toeing the ground, their hands buried in their pockets. One looks quizzically at the other, and above them stretch the words "You been farming long?" Their faces have the vague definition that children share with the very old. Their eyes are hidden under folds of skin as they squint.

/////

On April 22, 1865, a company of Union soldiers, on their way north to Fayetteville, vandalized a temperance hall that stood near a millpond in the northern reaches of what would become Lothian County, at a site just south of

Wayfare. In a field that rises a few hundred yards beyond the millpond, members of a temperance society had built an eight-sided hall where they could pray and celebrate their sober successes by painting on the ceiling gold stars emblematic of the faithful. When the Union soldiers came upon the hall, they destroyed its furniture, tore up the books and Bibles kept there, and dumped benches, books, and whatever else they felt like carting into the millpond. They must have thrown bottles at the ceiling, at that beautiful octagon constellated with gold stars. They must have had contests to see who could blot out the most stars with to-bacco spit. The pond where they threw the books and chairs was on land not two hundred yards from where James Leonade Clare, Archie's grandfather, would build his house.

The story of the soldiers at Temperance Hall is one that I hear over and over again at the Clare household. Something about the way it connects the land and family to history leads the Clares to select it for one of the first stories to tell new friends. Archie mentioned it again later that morning as we headed east toward Campbell County. He wanted to show me the places connected to the family history, and so we drove toward Fulton and the oldest cemetery in the county. Four miles east of Farlanboro we crossed a dip in the highway and Archie pulled to the side of the road. Cypress, tulip poplar, and black gum trees had gathered into their boughs a thick shade of mistletoe and waxy-leafed vines. We were looking at a small, isolated swamp that seemed like any other except for the huge trails of Spanish moss that grew on the tree limbs. Barney had jumped out of the truck to swim out into the black water beneath the bridge and snap at the bugs straddling the surface.

"This," said Archie, "is a Carolina bay. Some say that our area was hard to settle because of these depressions, but that's just a way to work a peculiar feature of the land into their stories. There are thousands of bays between here and the coast. They got their name from the bay trees that grow around them. They're full of peat. Oh, there are lots of stories about them, theories I suppose. Some people claim that they are old whale wallows left over from before the sea receded. Others think they're craters from a shower of meteors—all the bays are supposed to be situated on lines pointing from the northwest to the southwest. One thing is for sure, though, and that's that they gave Sherman's people fits when they tried to move through here. You'd think they would have had the sense to go around them." We got back in the truck and Barney shook off in the truck bed.

"The Murray land grant was over across the Lumber River north of Fulton. Duncan Murray had a daughter who married Archibald Wilson. The Murray family plot is over there on the other side of the river and has been since the beginning of the nineteenth century. But this Murray woman who married Wilson, her name was Margaret Wilson, she was the one that was tried for murder and released. She turned a slave out to kill a white man who was fooling around with one of her female slaves. Had the slave kill him with an ax. The courts let her go free—must have been late seventeen-hundreds, early eighteen-hundreds. But the trial was in Rockingham. They let her go because of the fact that she was protecting her property." He laughed. "I reckon had it been a man he probably wouldn't have given a damn, but a woman, she reckoned he was trying to take her property. She was set free. So Margaret Wilson was a slave owner.

"I reckon Margaret Wilson's husband Archibald had died. Margaret Wilson had a tremendous farm that she had gotten from her mother who was a Smith. The Smith woman would be my great-great-great—Lord, I don't know how many back she is. Anyway, she married Murray; Wilson married her daughter, Margaret, and the daughter of

Margaret and Archibald Wilson, Fanny Wilson, married my grandfather. The Murrays go way back. I reckon they were probably the first white people came to this part of the country, probably because they had a land grant. Murray Township—it's them that it's named for. They were Tories. So I don't know whether Whigs took the land or she lost it through bad times. Those dates are on the tombstone over there. Just before the road crosses the river, turn right on the first dirt road. Someone keeps the cemetery pretty well cleaned out."

The heat and the cigarette smoke in the truck made it hard to concentrate. What is there to do about family history? In the Clare household family stories constitute about half the daily conversation. The Clares turn to their family stories as if their lives depended on them. They never tire of presenting lists of names and places that create fuzzy, somnolent landscapes in the minds of their listeners, dreamy worlds inhabited by half-formed faces, like those of actors in old black-and-white movies that we saw when we were children.

I had discovered that there is no plot to a drought, just waiting, driving, diversion, and, of course, heat. I had been unable to witness Archie's work on the farm because drought had, in effect, evaporated all tasks he normally would have performed. But I had also found that a corollary to the heat's mind-numbing power was the family story itself. Everything that the summer heat had done to me seemed to be concentrated in the narratives told by Archie about his ancestors. When I found myself immersed in anecdotes about the old days and faces, I felt myself grow weary with the exhaustion produced by the successive generations of those individual lives, as if I had lived them myself. Can it be that family stories conjure up in us feelings parallel to those the ancestors felt during their battles, migrations, and little intersections with history?

Whatever the dynamic, a family history, with its stupefying details, works like a drug on the mind. At the Clares', whenever I found myself in the thicket of details and names, for some reason I always turned back to an image from a grade-school science textbook: a tiny red salamander emerging from the shiny sediment of river-bottom silt and muck. I found it very difficult to remember and imagine the details of my own ancestors' lives. But I didn't find it difficult to ask myself the question that arose from the Clares' accounts of their family history: What will they say about Archie Clare when he is gone?

/ / / / /

"Those grants were tremendous—whole townships owned by one family," Archie continued when we were back on the road. "I think that where lots of those people came into ownership is when the king of England went bankrupt, the earls and such turned against him, but finally he recouped and threw them out. Some of their holdings over here were probably done away with and dispersed to those loyal to the king. The grants didn't give total ownership, but gave the possessors the authority to reap the profits. I think the king could take what he granted back if he wanted to. I guess that's the way the royal family looked at it. Hell, that's the way it is here—if you don't pay your tax to the government, they'll take your land. So things haven't changed since feudal times in that respect. County tax now is a pretty big expense. Damn, you can't sell land even if you want to, that's the bad part—they got the value way out of reason when the land is practically worthless. But that Murray woman was right hell for most of the men. Her marriage to Wilson moved our family out of Drew County into Lothian. The Wilsons were pretty well established and they were pretty thickly Scots. There were cousins—MacKenzies—they were all Scottish. Murrays and Wilsons would have been English. Somewhere in there the ruling royalists in England and Germany were closely connected kin, but I don't know much about that.

"I suppose you could say on my grandmother's side they been here longer than any of my ancestors on the Clare side. Then too, my daddy's mother, she brought on all that, she married my grandfather, and their union brought the Murray-Wilson part of the family history into the rest of the story."

Archie had begun his family story with the ancestors who had lived in the Sandhills and inner coastal plain. He traced them back to the Murrays, whose presence in the area Archie associated with land grants from colonial times, through Fanny Wilson, his grandmother, who married James Leonade Clare from Hillsborough. As Archie spoke, I felt myself sifting through the words, searching for images that those words might restore.

"Now the Clare side. We don't know about the line beyond my great-grandfather, Charles Loveland Clare. Don't know anything more about him but his grave. The tombstone in Hillsborough says he came from Glastonbury, Connecticut. Came to North Carolina as a preacher, a Methodist, and apparently—well, I don't know anything that was written about it, but I assume he was a lay preacher. Eliza Ann, his wife, died about three years after him. You know, I believe he died shortly after the Civil War. His father was named Elihu, and his mother was Rhoda Clark. Now that's also on the gravestone. From Glastonbury, and that's about as far as anyone's ever gone as far as proof is concerned, except for the census record of Rhoda Clark being born in Connecticut.

"So this great-grandfather of mine, Charles Loveland Clare, was born on the twenty-ninth of July, 1794. He died in Hillsborough, North Carolina, between 1860 and 1870. His wife was Eliza Ann Chapman, born 1806 in North Carolina. Their children were Thomas Lemay, 1829, Mary Katty, 1832, Amanda Ann, 1834, William Jabber, 1835 (William was the church historian in Hillsborough), Archibald Sterling, 1839, James Leonade, 1842 (now that was my grandfather), and Joseph Gaston Brown Clare, 1846."

As he drove, Archie put on his glasses and looked at a paper on which he had transcribed the names and dates from the family Bible. The truck slowed to fifteen miles per hour, and Archie would occasionally jerk the wheel to steer the truck back to the road after it had wandered onto the shoulder. He recited the names and descriptions with a matter-of-fact tone, the way a priest chants the liturgy, as if the words were so familiar that we scarcely need to be reminded of them.

"Now that isn't even all of Charles Loveland Clare's children. According to the entries in our family Bible he had one, two, three, four, five, six, seven, eight, nine, ten, eleven. And according to the Bible there is an Emilia Eliza, and another daughter, Mary Cain. There was another called Caroline Matilda, and there was another, Temesia. Now those three women married in Hillsborough—to men by the names of Harris, Colburn, and East. Amanda Ann married a Hardaway."

Archie had a way of treating the names as if they referred to friends from grade school whose faces and personalities he knew well. His comments touched on his ancestors' lives with a familiarity that resembled in an odd way the casual fixing of a collar, straightening of a tie, and brushing of a son's sports coat shoulders that a father might perform before sending his boy off to a dance.

"So four girls married and the rest were Clares, men. Also the Bible lists Thomas Lemay, oldest son, who died in New York City. And then William Jabber, who died in 1904 in Rowland, North Carolina. He didn't marry. Archibald Sterling—doesn't give when he died, but he lived in Hillsborough. James Leonade Clare who married Fanny Wilson, my grandmother. Joseph Gaston Brown Clare—why he had four names, I don't know—who moved to Sandersville, Georgia. James Leonade Clare, William Jabber Clare, and Joseph Gaston Brown Clare were evidently the only ones that ever had children. Archibald never did. Joseph Gaston Brown's son Lonnie went to Colorado and married Mary Molly Shelly—that's from the census and also the Bible. I don't know what happened to him. I reckon he died out there. His other children were druggists—two in Sanderville, Arthur in Fulton. William Jabber Clare had a son. He died in Charlotte not long ago. I met him once. He came by to see my aunts, who were his first cousins. He made money in dye mills in Charlotte. He was driving a Cadillac. Charles Loveland Clare's sons all fought in the Civil War, and they all survived the war. They all fought for the Confederacy, which is a bit of a shock considering they were only first-generation Southerners."

I had not been able to keep straight the family lines and connections, and the names of the eleven Clare children didn't help me make sense of the story. Archie's narration served as an epic catalog, giving substance and weight to a family's history in a place through its insistent flurry of details. It seemed that whatever value resided in the review of family history lay precisely in the recitation. Through the performance itself Archie participated in the mysteries of his origins, in the network of causes and effects that located him in his place and time.

"There are no certain records of the Clares in Glastonbury except that Rhoda turns up in the 1820 census. A fellow named Aaron Clare lived there the same time as

Rhoda, but we don't know what the connection was, probably a brother of Elihu. A number of Clares settled in Springfield, Massachusetts. Eliza Ann Chapman was a Cape Fear Scot—that link between Hillsborough and Glastonbury is in the Bible and on the tombstone."

Archie had turned north on an unmarked road and said that we would head toward Wayfare.

"Charles Loveland Clare was my great-grandfather. James Leonade Clare was my grandfather and John Leonade Clare was my father. James Leonade Clare, my grandfather, lived from 1842 to 1912 and was a member of Company Six, Twenty-seventh North Carolina Troops, attached to the Army of Northern Virginia. The story on him, he and his brothers left Hillsborough together to become Confederate soldiers. All of them went through the war. And the remarkable thing is that they all survived it. How James Leonade Clare got here was he was released in Wilmington as a prisoner of the Union. He was captured in the war and he was in a prison camp in Virginia. My brother John, he's also John Leonade Clare named after my father, has a list of the battles our grandfather fought in. He was in one of the companies that fought at Gettysburg, but he wasn't in Gettysburg at the time of the big battle. He and others were off raiding trains. I believe he was with that general who raided trains in Maryland, the one who worked his way all the way to Maine raiding trains, robbing banks, and stealing horses."

While Archie had succeeded in conveying that the generations that preceded him were densely populated, I was unable to assimilate the significance of any but the broadest outline. Archie's great-grandfather, Charles Loveland Clare, had moved to Hillsborough, North Carolina, from Connecticut. And he had a large family. And all of his sons fought against the Union and survived.

A glance at the bookshelves in the Clare home revealed that Archie was an avid reader of Civil War history. His preoccupation with his family's remote past seemed to focus on the various intersections between the public story of the nation and the obscure world of Lothian County. The Civil War had clearly captured his imagination. Perhaps it was because the war, related according to the surviving attitudes of the Confederacy, had still been the news when he was a boy. Coming to terms with the war had represented the mystery, the worry, and the business of adulthood, the facts of the real world as he had imagined them to be.

"Right after the war the Union soldiers loaded their Confederate prisoners on a boat. I'm not sure where James Leonade Clare had really been kept in prison, maybe as far north as Maryland or even Delaware or Pennsylvania. Anyway, the Union sent their prisoners to Wilmington to release them. After he arrived in Wilmington and was released, James Leonade Clare walked on the railroad line from Wilmington to Farlanboro—a hundred miles. His company commander was Captain Charles McFarland, whom they called Captain Charlie, under A. P. Hill. McFarland is the one Farlanboro was named after. Used to be McFarlanboro, but that was too much of a mouthful and so some of the letters got dropped over the years. Well, James Leonade Clare was trying to meet up with his company commander, Captain Charlie, and for some reason he didn't go home to Hillsborough. So that's how he got here. He married Captain Charlie's daughter, Mary Katty. Her grave is out at Scottsville Cemetery. She died childless two years after she and James Leonade Clare got married.

"After Mary Katty's death, James Leonade Clare moved to Wayfare. And when he moved to Wayfare he got up with this Wilson woman over there, Fanny Wilson, and he married her. And that's where my father and all his brothers and sisters came, through Fanny Wilson. My grandfather lived to be pretty old. There were only two rooms in the house he built, the room with the fireplace in it and the room next to that. Fanny Wilson, the second woman James Clare married, well, her mother and father had a tremendous house right across the road from where James Clare built his. We're coming up to that property now."

Where the Wilson house had stood, across the road from one of the Clares', we found a stand of black gums and oaks. Archie pointed out two mulberries at the head of what used to be the lane leading to the house. Mulberries were fashionable for a time during the late nineteenth century when a man in south Lothian tried to raise silkworms and imported hundreds of the trees before failure or distraction led him to other things. Archie pointed out where the barn had been. Now broken bricks, glass, and gravel littered the hollow where the house, surrounded by willow oaks, had stood.

"When Fanny Wilson had all these children, her mother and father must have helped to raise them. Old Man Murray, Fanny Wilson's grandfather, he had slaves. He was a farmer and I believe he had two slaves, a man and a woman. Some of those colored Wilsons are still over there around Wayfare. There was one colored Wilson who was a carpenter. My granddaddy Clare got him to build him a barn.

"Fanny Wilson, I believe she had one sister only. I don't believe there were any men in her family. They had lots of cousins down at Watertown on the river. The Wilson house burned not too long ago. In the seventies. When I was a boy, Cousin Will owned it. That's Will Scott. You know Will Scott, who helped us when we ran out of gas the other day. Will Scott got the Wilson house from his uncle, the way he got everything else. It was inhabited from time to time by vagrants and other people who had nowhere else to live. Colored McRaes lived there for a time. They worked for Waynette's family cutting trees in the woods. And then there was another black woman whose name I cannot recall."

Archie shook his head as he let go of the attempt to bring back her name and story. There were always people associated with the main line of Archie's narratives who had slipped out of his grasp. The way Archie handled the memories of the people he talked about made me wonder who was keeping memories of the people on the peripheries of his stories alive.

"Back then J. J. Flaxman, he was what you would call an entrepreneur. He bought the Wilson house from Will Scott and began to restore it. He had some big ideas. He bought it and the barn and then tore the barn down to use the lumber. That was good lumber—some of the boards from that barn on the Wilson land are right there in our kitchen floor. He was going to move out there. He lived in Wayfare while he was fixing up the Wilson place. There had always been a gigantic sycamore tree in the Wilson's front yard. Flaxman had a tree surgeon to cut the top part out of it. He had hay stacked in the house. Right about that time, when he was tending to the sycamore, lightning struck the house, set it on fire, and burned it right down, all the way to the ground right quick.

"And that was a shame, because this house was one of the oldest houses in the entire county. It was standing when Sherman came through and some of Sherman's crowd killed some Confederates in the yard. The Confederates had camped there. As Sherman moved up from Cheraw, one spearhead moved along Old Wire Road. Others came from Sumter. They bogged down in that creek that runs along and then crosses Route 151 south of Wayfare. They had an encampment there in what would become the

Wayfare graveyard, stayed a few days, then moved up to Fayetteville with Johnston. At the time there were invalids in the Wilson house, and one of the sisters was tending them, so the Union forces didn't burn it down. They let it go. Wayfare wasn't much of a town then, and they let the house stand."

We got back into the truck and drove down the highway a few hundred yards before passing the house where Archie's brother John lived. We proceeded a bit farther until we turned onto the drive to the old Clare house. The roof had fallen in on the west side and huge magnolias grew up like columns at the front of the house. The Clares called it the "new" house, but Archie's father had built it long after Archie's grandfather had built the other house. When Archie's father got married, he built the old house so that he could raise his own family on the Clare land. Archie's aunts, Pearl and Rose, continued to live in the house that their father, James Leonade Clare, had built. Eventually Archie's father added some rooms to his father's house and Archie's brother moved in to raise his family there.

As we drove down the sand road that ran between the two Clare houses, I was struck by the lack of activity. It looked like nobody was home in either house. The absence of the current residents underscored Archie's omission of them from his narratives. Seeing the houses allowed me to understand why they had been assigned names that contradicted their history. James Leonade Clare, Archie's grandfather, built the first house at the southern end of the millpond. It was modest, without ostentatious columns and having only one upstairs room. Now Archie's brother and his family lived in that house, which they called the "new" house. When I compared it to the second house built on the property, the old house, I could see that the misnomers, in fact, accurately described the appearance of the houses. The old house had been built according to a grander style, with prominent columns in the front, an elaborate second story that presented intricate lines where the various gables intersected.

As I surveyed the Clare farm, I saw that it possessed all the elements of the idealized family farm, the Farm as I had always pictured it when I was a boy. Along the side and running nearly the length of the new house was a screened-in porch with two rocking chairs on it. The porch looked out toward a small group of hardwoods that gave way to a thick growth of pines. Behind the house stood a chicken coop, a hog pen, a barn that housed the tractors and pulls; beyond the outbuildings lay the millpond. This summer no crops were growing in the field between the two Clare houses, although it had been plowed into rows that were now covered with brown weeds.

I knew that John, the oldest brother, lived in the new house with his three sons and two daughters, that he raised cattle, hogs, tobacco, wheat, corn, and beans. Archie's brother Billy had continued to live in the old house with his mother long after John and Maggie and Archie had moved out, and he remained there after his mother died. It was believed that Billy led a rough life, although no one in the Clare family seemed to know much about what he did, not even Archie. Apparently Billy had cattle on land up in the Sandhills from time to time, and he may have spent most of his days tending to or merely watching his cows. Billy had let the Clare house fall down around him, and the caved-in roof and broken windows fostered the impression that Billy was a haunting presence in the house. As I thought about how strange it must have been for Archie to visit his childhood home and the property that he had simply given up, Archie directed my thoughts to the more distant past by carrying on with the story of his grandfather.

Archie had stopped the truck at the edge of the millpond where we surveyed the dozens of gray cypress stumps that poked above the surface of the water. From where we sat we could see both of the Clare houses, the outbuildings, and the fields and woods that surrounded the heart of the Clare land. Turtles poked their heads through the surface of the pond, looking like stones hovering on the water. If we continued down the road by the millpond, Archie told me, we would soon come to old Temperance Hall.

"When James Leonade Clare got to Wayfare, being a harness maker and having a shop, somehow or other he also carried mail. There was a crossroad post office at Wayfare that at the time was called by some Scottish name, and he ran it. So I reckon at the turn of the century he made it on his own and he was postmaster until he died. Pearl, his daughter, was postmistress after him until she retired. That was two generations that Clares were in the postal business. His children married into the Scots, Minceys, Pedens, Swopes in Virginia, and Hollieway, and then there were two old maids, my aunts, Rose and Pearl, the postmistress, who stayed on here at the farm until they died. One of James's sons, my uncle Robert, was nearly killed in a horse accident. He was driving a team that ran away and he got caught under them or the wagon and was dragged a long way. He survived, but then while he was recovering they found out he had tuberculosis and that was the end of him. He had to live his last days out in a tent on this land. He died real young. I think Daddy was then about twelve or thirteen. Grandpa lived till 1912 or 1913. Daddy was born in 1898. He must have been fifteen, then, when his father died. My father was left to take care of his mother, Fanny. His sister Mary Katty married Dr. Scott. My grandmother Fanny had decided she would name her first daughter after James's first wife, Mary Katty. Two of James Leonade

Clare's children were dead by the time he died. Aunt Sally married before Daddy, but Daddy married late in life, in his forties. He was left with his mother, three of the girls, and one brother, so he built onto the house five more rooms for the girls."

Following Archie's words was one thing; putting them together into a coherent story was another. As name followed name, the sequence possessed an immediate logic and coherence that was ultimately deceptive. For when the names and relationships had accumulated I was no longer certain that I had learned much of anything about the family. I started to recognize a familiar pattern in my ramblings with Archie Clare: he was seeing things that were invisible to me. Once more, a place that appeared to me to be deserted was crowded in Archie's mind with the names and faces of the past. I may have lost the thread of Archie's family story, but I had gained a sense of how rich and wonderful were the human images Archie superimposed upon the various sites that defined the circuit of his life.

"That brings it up-to-date. After that John Leonade Clare married my mother and lived in the family house for a year until he finished the house that Billy lives in now, what we call the old house. Mother was from Durham County and was a schoolteacher. She taught in the county system, and my father's sister, Aunt Leah, taught in the city system. After my mother got married she didn't teach anymore. My grandfather had bought about fifty acres of land and added it to Fanny's inheritance of thirty-two, thirty-three acres. She didn't own much land. So my grandfather was a farmer and all that; anyway, he had to be to make a living and feed all those children. When he was about sixty-seven he died in his sleep.

"But my grandfather never forgot the war when he grew old. The story that my daddy used to tell was that old

James Leonade Clare had gone to a convention in New York that was a reunion of both North and South armies. I don't know if Captain Charlie McFarland was dead then or not. There was supposedly an article in the Farlanboro newspaper about it. James Leonade Clare took his Confederate flag with him even though it was against the law to fly the Confederate flag and to display Robert E. Lee's photograph. He took that Confederate flag with him, believe it or not, and he made a big scene by raising it up and shouting. That part made the papers. The officials at the convention didn't do anything about it—it had all been just in fun.

"I remember that he had brought home a battle flag of the Twenty-seventh Light Infantry under A. P. Hill, and I have seen it. I think all his brothers were in the same outfit. How they didn't get killed I don't know. Just lucky. But when you think about it, that's some accomplishment, five boys from one family all fighting in and all *surviving* the Civil War. And it could be too that they were the ones that fired on Stonewall Jackson at night in the swamp and killed him, thinking he was Union cavalry."

I wondered if that thought had just occurred to Archie or if he had evidence that linked James Leonade Clare to Stonewall Jackson. Archie continued before I had formulated my doubts well enough to raise the question.

"Oh, my grandfather told stories about the war and handed them down. The stories came to me from my daddy and my aunts. James Leonade Clare chewed tobacco and kept six plugs and a Bible in his coat pocket. There's a bullet hole in the Bible that he was supposed to have had in his pocket during a battle, and the Bible saved him from the bullet—that's hearsay. Otherwise he didn't get hit or lose any limbs. Managed to stay alive. After the war he had a beard down past his chest to his beltline. It was gray. So I guess he had peculiar ways.

"Over here at John's house, one day when they were cleaning, they took a painting off the wall and it fell away from its frame. On the back side of the painting they found a portrait of Robert E. Lee. The portrait had been turned around backward and someone had painted on the other side. I don't know if that was my grandfather's way of rebelling, of refusing to stop the war in his own mind, or if he just didn't have any use for the portrait of Lee and let someone use it to paint another picture. That way he could have kept a picture of his hero even though it would have been illegal to do so.

"The Union let the Confederate prisoners keep their weapons and clothing when they were released. That's all James Leonade Clare had when he came this way. I guess he had picked up harness making in Hillsborough before the war. One brother, Archibald Sterling Clare, made cabinets and he made beds out of walnut. My son, Alec, has one of his beds now. Horse work might be what saved my grandfather's life—maybe he was tending to the horses when things got dangerous during the war. There weren't many who lived through the war that long. He would a been about eighteen when he went to war, but was probably nineteen by the time he fought. It took the war a year to get going. South Carolina was the first and North Carolina was the last to secede except Kentucky, and Kentucky never did anything. Fighting didn't actually start until 1861 —Lee had to get his army together, you see. Practically all of the Confederate officers had originally been in the Union army, and they were given a choice as to which they wanted to be in. So all of the Confederates were West Pointers—more West Pointers in the Confederate army than in the Union. Stanton and Lincoln couldn't get along with West Point officers. The Union leaders would give them a chance, but after they lost a battle—

and they didn't start winning any until 1863 — they'd be fired.

"James Leonade Clare lived from 1842 to 1912 and was a member of Company Six, Twenty-seventh North Carolina troops, attached to the Army of Virginia. And of course there's the good and the bad from the war that we're still living with. The worst is taxes and the growth of the federal government. That has its source in the victory of the Union forces."

/ / / / /

Archie finished his account of his grandfather and started the truck, pulling back onto the highway toward Farlanboro. The heat and the words of the day had exhausted me. Archie fell silent after commenting that it was past lunchtime and he was ready for his nap. So as we drove I fell into my reverie and pieced together some of the scraps of the past that I'd accumulated.

War would have made James Leonade Clare's hands resemble Archie's even in James's early twenties. Sunlight, war, leaving home—all these would have worn, aged, and toughened them. He would have had the same curve to his forearm, the same light scattering of black hair as Archie. And when he was released from the Union prison, shipped to Wilmington, and let go, he would have made the same overland trek that the Highlanders had made between 1792 and 1819, the years of the main Scottish migration from coastal Carolina to the blank interior. The story goes that the early Scots found a sign posted on a road at the western edge of Wilmington that read: "The best land lies 100 miles west of here."

James Leonade Clare walked the Old One Hundred, along the unfinished tracks of what would become famous for being the longest straight stretch of railroad tracks in the world when it was completed sometime after the Civil War. Perhaps without knowing it he retraced the very route the Scots had walked, orienting himself in the more traditional way to a region his own family had discovered after coming south from Connecticut. And he must have found the new perspective that his return to North Carolina afforded him commodious, despite the grinding effort of the million steps he had to take to reach Farlanboro. He would have crossed the region of lakes just west of Wilmington, where the terrain was so flat that he wouldn't have seen any water until he nearly stumbled into it. He would have tried to conserve the tobacco given to him by some sympathetic citizen as he disembarked in Wilmington. He would have seen lots of Indians, many of whom were making the same journey inland from Wilmington, where they had been enslaved along with blacks to build the last rebel defense.

What did this preacher's son, whose daddy would have told him stories of ice-skating in Connecticut, what did he think about going home? Either he knew he would never return to his home in Hillsborough and to his father, or he walked a hundred miles making up his mind. Maybe he determined after a hundred miles that home was not enough. Maybe someone who stayed behind during the war had won the affections of James's sweetheart. Even though she sewed the buttons from one of James's uniforms onto her wedding dress, even though the buttons from his uniform gleamed like wet gravel against her white gown, she married a man who never went to war. Maybe James Leonade Clare's sweetheart married a man whose course lay nearer to her own and whose beliefs agreed with hers. Maybe she was against the war. Or maybe it had been her despair at his capture that led her to try to cut him out of her memory. Maybe she could not bear the thought that James Leonade

Clare would probably die like the rest of the boys, that waiting to find out would be almost as intolerable as James's being forced to sit idle in a prison camp during a war that only dead men could win or find their way home from. Maybe it was that James simply no longer wrote to her and could not face her after years of silence. Or maybe it was a letter written by her that he found by accident when looking for tobacco in his brother's pack, a letter in script as familiar and bittersweet as pine smoke.

One hundred miles from the known world into the shadowy precincts under the green of the piney woods are the obscure haunts of the Tuscarora and the Lumbee Indians. And how would he know when he found the home of his subsequent generations? Would it be the sad absence of concern for the things of the civilized world, would it be being caught and balanced between the full moon rising and full sun setting in a storm of pine pollen? Would it be the sound of a preacher's Gaelic in full bloom among rafters of a nearly empty church, a decongregated congregation that would have said to this man full of war and tobacco and straight mile after mile: "This is a stranger place for all its sameness than wherever your father fled and his father before him. No one can take from here this wilderness of culture, these tartan-wrapped altars, these Presbyterian epistles, these exhausting miles, these ruined turpentine manufactures, these desolating weathers, these hidden indolences."

And then there was Captain Charlie McFarland, giving his name to a place. And there was Captain Charlie's daughter, who made James's thoughts scatter and dip like feeding swallows in evening air and who made light itself split into particles and fall between the pines like snowflakes. And what kind of return was it, in fact, to search for Captain Charlie in the piney woods? It was a return to absence,

to being not at home. It made sense for this train raider to
walk one hundred miles on railroad tracks and set his home
on the Old Wire Road, a place where distance and absence
would always seem to be the measure of experience. Maybe the train raider, the preacher's son, the Confederate,
came to a place that was important to him for what it was
not. When he settled he married a woman who would soon
die. It would seem to him that he was always marrying
himself to whatever died: home, the South, the war, Mary
Katty. But he stayed put after Mary Katty died, married
Fanny Wilson, started a post office in Wayfare, and delivered letters to and from faraway places.

/ / / / /

The Scots clustered around a couple of places in the region: the areas that would become Farlanboro, Mulberries
Hill, and Wayfare. Until 1834 Gaelic masses were standard
at David Barclay's church in Wayfare. He preached two
sermons; one was in English, the other in Gaelic. An annual
Scottish trade fair was held near the site of the Mulberries
Hill Presbyterian Church, where for over a hundred years
before James Leonade Clare arrived the Scots had traded
and sold their produce, livestock, and wares. The fair drew
merchants from as far north as Fayetteville who traveled
down the "chicken road," named for the flocks of chickens
driven to market, and from as far south as Cheraw, South
Carolina. The trade fair must have resembled the contemporary county fairs of North Carolina and included ath-
letic contests, horse races, and gambling. The fair had accumulated its own traditions, and the traders and card
players who participated in the fair's activities knew that
in the very old days their counterparts had used English,
French, and Spanish coins that were often halved and quar-
tered. Even in James Leonade Clare's time there would

have been jokes about using newfangled American money, which had been accepted at the fair only after 1800.

When James Leonade Clare arrived, industry was scarce in the Farlanboro region. First there was Ross Mill, west of Farlanboro. John Aiken had established a gun shop in Blackgum Swamp, which was moved just before the Civil War to Ross Mill, where Fergus Conill established a gun factory that produced twenty-five guns a week until Sherman's troops destroyed it. After the war Captain Charles Hurry started a cotton mill there. Cotton would be a major crop until after James Leonade Clare's time, until the nineteen-fifties, when machinery would give more readily industrialized crops the edge. By the nineteen-twenties and thirties melons and cantaloupes would become an enormous crop in the region.

In 1840 only four houses stood in Farlanboro. But when James Leonade Clare turned up in Farlanboro in 1865, he saw the beginnings of a boom town. The Carolina Central Railroad shops were located there, and the railroad traffic contributed not only to the economy but also to the social life. Farlanboro was gaining a reputation as a wild town with a fun-loving, heavy-drinking populace. In 1877 the town incorporated. In 1901 Farlanboro underwent a major restructuring, and it is through records of the town's deconstruction that we can see what it had become by the turn of the century. According to newspaper accounts, soon after its incorporation Farlanboro had a courthouse and a jail that constituted the presence of government in the town. For society there was a hotel called the Cottonland, a barbershop, a Western Union office, two men's shops, two clothing stores owned and operated by Warren Dunbar, and a small café. Holding society together were a watch repair shop, a produce market, a fish market, a storage building, a junk heap, and a sheet metal shop. Right downtown was a Negro church. The Presbyterian and Methodist churches lay on the periphery of the business section. Renovation of the business district involved the destruction of several slum houses. None of the newspaper accounts mentions the names of the taverns or their owners. The Carolina Central Railroad shops left in 1894 and moved to a small town, Manley, thirty miles west. The Farlanboro residents planted sycamores and elms on the residential streets, and, judging from what survives, they must also have planted lots of willow oak.

Between James Leonade Clare and his old home in Hillsborough lay the barren wastes of the Sandhills, and it wouldn't be until after his death that the Sandhills would emerge from obscurity. A lot of lumber remained in the area at the turn of the century, but most of it was logged soon after that, and scrub and blackjack oak took over. In 1895 the first peach was planted in the Sandhills, and by 1923 four million peach trees flourished on ground that previously had been considered so poor that it was only good for holding the world together. Businessmen from the north, J. W. Tufts and J. T. Patrick, through independent efforts developed Pinehurst in the northern Sandhills into a resort town that boasted more housing capacity than any city between Washington and Atlanta.

Economic growth and the introduction of a tourist trade into the region naturally fueled the celebration of cultural traditions, both indigenous and those imported from Europe. In 1918 as many as three fox hunts a week, fifty a season, took place in Moore County. Wearing scarlet coats, navy-blue collars, brass buttons, yellow vests, white stockings, silk top hats, white breeches and black boots, garter straps and spurs, the hunters raced through the woods and over the sand plains. The area around Pinehurst and Southern Pines became devoted to the cultivation of peaches, grapes, dewberries, beans, tomatoes, and pimentos. The Sandhills businesses launched an advertising campaign in the big state newspapers in the twenties and thirties. Articles in the Raleigh and Greensboro newspapers offered headlines like "Amazing Development of Once Barren Sand Hills of State," "4,000,000 Peach Trees in Bloom Bring Glory to Sandhills of N.C.," "Sandhills Area Is Thriving and Moving Section," and "Sandhills Built from Barren Waste to Winter Resort Famed Throughout Civilized World." The region's most serious assault on fame was reported in an article appearing on August 30, 1946: "Sandhills Under Serious Consideration as Future Home of United Nations."

The metropolis envisioned by those pushing the area as a site for the United Nations, a site that seemed ideal to those who considered golf to be the essential medium for diplomacy, never materialized. Several other attempts to secure a place on the map came with the establishment of sanatoriums by individuals convinced of the restorative properties of pine air and spring water. But the lumber business, tobacco farming, and truck farming continued to be the mainstays of the economy.

As early as 1947 one newspaper article answered its own question—"What do the people of the Sandhills live on?"—in the following fashion: "Rich Yankees in winter, peaches in summer, tobacco in the fall with some cotton and truck." By 1953 only two wintertime hotels survived in the Sandhills. On March 1, 1960, thirty inches of snow fell in Southern Pines. It had all melted by March 8.

James Leonade Clare would have seen the drought that began in 1897, and sometime during the nights of February fifteenth, sixteenth, or later on that week, had he looked into the sky he would have seen a tremendous orange glow in the north and west, perhaps even seen showers of sparks bursting into the sky. That winter a freak wind blew into southern Chatham County and the northern Sandhills. The wind and a hunter's stray bullet ignited some rusty pine straw, and then the yellow hummocks of wire grass. Eventually the blaze exploded the turpentine from the naval stores. The fire burned all the way through seven counties in North Carolina and ten in South Carolina, consuming a hundred thousand acres in just hours. Trees exploded in the heat, which tore the spikes from railroad tracks and left the rails twisted like snakes.

SEVEN

BY THE TIME Archie and I had returned home and eaten lunch, the race of the dinner pans and dishes was on. Archie retired to his room to take a nap. After dinner I promised that I would do the dishes later if Waynette would tell me about her family.

"Did I ever tell about the time my father was cured by a bunch of grapes in France? This story is my father's, Robert Wallace's. My father was in the expeditionary forces in France after the war. Yes, that's World War One." Waynette focused immediately on the stories of those she knew personally. Archie had said little about his father, his brothers, and his sister. His mind roamed where his imagination had freedom to play, but Waynette preferred the charm of the familiar.

I suppose that any woman in Lothian County who was married to a farmer and who claimed that Albert Camus was her favorite author might be considered interesting, if not peculiar. Yet even though Waynette was married to a farmer and did enjoy Camus, there was nothing contradictory about her. In fact, I'm not sure that I have ever met another person with as much self-assurance as Waynette appeared to have. I had never seen her lose her temper. She was almost always genuinely cheerful, and when she was annoyed by one of Archie's habits or oversights, she expressed herself with a detached humor that seemed to feign exasperation rather than convey it. It might be said that Waynette Clare was perfectly proper and nearly flawless.

She was the kind of person about whom people would say, "If there's anything bad about Waynette, it could only be that she's too nice."

Waynette stood about five feet eight inches and had preserved a youthful thinness into her middle age. In her mid-fifties, she was energetic and lively. Once, after having brought a colleague home for lunch one day, I heard him remark about both of the Clares: "They are handsome, and they are *fit*." Waynette was extremely articulate and pronounced her words crisply and delicately. But, oddly, her southern accent seemed much more pronounced than Archie's. She was usually meticulously dressed and almost always wore dresses or skirts, although on some of the hottest days she wore shorts and short-sleeved cotton shirts if she was going to spend any time at all outside. She insisted that the house be comfortably cool. Some days Archie would bring home a watermelon and place it over the air-conditioning vent in the kitchen to cool it. Waynette found this practice intolerable since it barely cooled the watermelon but effectively blocked the chill air from entering the kitchen.

Waynette had her hair done every Thursday, standing appointment. Unlike Archie, she maintained a regular social life that included bridge once a week, volunteer work at a rest home once a week, and fairly regular teas and outings with various friends. Waynette had established a ritual orderliness to her daily routine. The order was most clearly manifested through her elaborate preparations for lunch and supper, which were always formal affairs that took place at tables with place-settings and linen napkins. I quickly discovered that failure to use a butter knife would earn her obvious but unspoken disapproval, and I noticed that Archie almost always shaved and changed his clothes before evening supper.

I had been somewhat surprised by Waynette's candor and the absence of prudery in her discussion of the lives and concerns of her students and in her comments about current social problems. She had been teaching French for twenty-five years in the public schools and she had seen education go through many changes. She would talk earnestly about the poor preparation many of her students had received, she deplored the increase in violence among the students, and she was outdone with the expansion of the administrative bureaucracy at the high school. It was often difficult to get Waynette to sit down and talk because she insisted on scurrying around the house polishing and putting up the silver or hunting down fallen ashes from Archie's cigarettes with the Dustbuster. She always wore an apron when she performed housework. Despite her observation of many of the domestic rituals associated with an old-world, male-dominated household, Waynette was a well-educated, well-read professional who had the income and the inclination to do precisely what she wanted.

That evening we left the kitchen after clearing the table and sat in the living room. "Originally my father had signed up for the air force," she began, "but they wouldn't take him because he had flat feet. So he went into the infantry and actually fought in Germany before the war was over." Waynette laughed, saying that it was hilarious to think that flat feet had landed her father in the infantry.

"There was a flu epidemic throughout Europe in 1918 and millions of people died from it. Daddy caught the flu—it might have been because he was fighting in the trenches—and he became so sick he couldn't move. The army placed him in a field hospital, which means that it was just a tent in a field. There were so many wounded from the war that all the indoor facilities were chock-full, and they certainly couldn't do much for you if all you had was flu while there were other boys around you with open wounds and the like. Well, one day Daddy got to feeling like he could get up and so he did. He walked outside. When he told the story to us he used to make such a big deal out of how it was a sunny day after many days of rain. Daddy wandered outside and went to sit down under an enormous tree. While he was sitting there a Frenchman, a peasant, with a big cart full of grapes came by and Daddy bought a bunch of grapes from him. He ate the grapes and stayed out there under the tree for a long time. He fell asleep for a while and when he woke up he felt great—he had been healed. He said that he just picked up and walked back to his infantry unit without even letting the hospital know that he was leaving. He was in army ordnance and corporal was as high a rank as he got."

She went into the kitchen to get a cup of coffee, and then returned to her seat and continued. "I don't know much about the Wallace side of the family, my daddy's side. Now Mama's side, the McKays, I know better since I grew up in almost daily contact with them. There are two old McKay homes in Moore County, in the Southern Pines area. We've been to see them. Alan McKay was my great-great-grandfather. His sons served in the Civil War. Grandfather, Hugh McKay, was a young man during Reconstruction. I don't know how it was he didn't have a great deal of formal education. He was one of four children. My great-grandfather's family were into naval stores, which is really just turpentine, but they also got interested in timber and logging and Grandfather made a whole lot of money at logging. They also lived in Cheraw, South Carolina. Grandfather would go to the logging camps on Monday and come back home Saturday. He bought a lot of land around Charleston and was one of the first to work the Okefenokee in southern Georgia. He wanted to move to Savannah, but the family wouldn't.

"Grandfather, he was principal owner of the logging camps. McKay Lumber. A young man took up with him, Duncan Armstrong. Granddaddy's children sold out to Armstrong. Granddaddy started out by working the woods himself. He bought a whole lot of land during the Depression. He had sawmills and planing mills and sold finished lumber. All the lumber in the house on Main Street where I grew up came from his mills. He built it for Mama and Daddy. By the time we got to the generation of Archie and me, class didn't matter. But both of our grandfathers built their fortunes, and both the Clare side and my side wanted their children to have an education. My grandfather sent one of his sons to medical school and his daughter to college and he offered education to all nine of his children. Most of them got married or for one reason or another were distracted from college. Before my grandfather built the house in Fulton—that's just over the line into Campbell County—he lived at his mill. Then in 1913 he built the house in Fulton that became the family house, you know, the center of gravity for the next few generations. All of the children but my aunt Rebecca had been born by then so she was the only one born in that house."

Archie walked in from the porch where he had been smoking and said good night. "I think it's sad that a man doesn't care any more about things than that, than to go to bed in the evening when people are talking." I couldn't tell if Waynette was just trying to assure me that if I thought Archie was being unsociable, she thought so too, or if she was really upset with him. She said it in her tone of false aggravation, and she said it with a smile.

"My grandfather died in 1940 or forty-one. I was about eleven or twelve. We thought he was simply marvelous, my cousins and I. He was . . . well, he enjoyed his grandchildren a lot and he would always tease us. There were sixteen of us first cousins and sometimes we'd all be over at Grand-father's house in Fulton at the same time. He'd walk into a room where some of us were playing and walk right up to us, looking at something over our heads, and then he'd look down at us like he was shocked to see us. He had an office in that flatiron building in Fulton. His office was on the second floor in the corner. Well, we'd all go walking downtown and we'd climb the stairs in the building and knock on the door to his office. He would give us nickels so we could run across the street to the drugstore and buy ice-cream cones. We'd say, 'Hey, Granddaddy!' and he'd hold out his arms like he hadn't seen us in years and he'd give us all nickels and when we got home we'd want to go back and do it all over again, and sometimes we did.

"My father was the youngest of nine. He lived with Archie and me for two years after Mama died. His father was a farm manager. I never knew much about that grand-father. Daddy grew up in Fulton on the same block as my mama's family. When Daddy came back from the war he worked in a bank in Fulton until the first time the banks closed before the Depression, in the twenties. Before the De-pression, wealthy men could pool their money and form a bank. Grandfather Wallace sent Daddy to Charlotte to business school. He was real good in math. I can tell you I went to school with all the answers in arithmetic and I didn't know how I'd gotten them. Daddy's bank also closed, so he went to a bank in Farlanboro in 1929. He had already been living in Farlanboro. The bank he worked for eventu-ally was bought by the bank that later became Wachovia."

Waynette's narrative just barely touched on the lives of people she hadn't known personally. She let the enigma of Grandfather Wallace alone in part because she seemed so much to enjoy having the opportunity to recall her childhood.

"When I was a little girl I'd ride a bus or a train back and forth from Farlanboro to Fulton for a dime. I would go over there to spend Friday nights. When I was *real* little, I would go spend the night with my aunt who ran a boardinghouse in Fulton. She ran her boardinghouse and she kept books for a hardware store. You could do fine in those days without a car. There were trains everywhere and it seems a shame that somebody's gone and torn all those tracks up.

"Daddy worked in the bank all those years until I was a senior in college, when he contracted tuberculosis. That was when the doctors had just started to find the cures for TB and drugs to treat the symptoms. Even so, he had to stay in sanatoriums for eighteen months. All the sanatoriums around Farlanboro were full and we couldn't get him in one, so we sent him to one up in Guilford by Greensboro for six months. Then he was able to get a room in one in the Sandhills for about a year. A year and a half after he came home he went back to work at the bank and he worked until he retired."

Waynette paused to ask me if I didn't want to start on the dishes. I assured her that I would do them, but I wanted to hear more about her life first.

"I wasn't suggesting that you would simply abandon the dishes," she said and laughed.

"I went to Queens College, in Charlotte, right after high school," she continued. "I just really fit the mold like the girls in the fifties did, except it was the forties. I went to Queens for four years and did volunteer work in the summers. I was a counselor at a Girl Scout camp for our church at Cheraw Beach in South Carolina. The weather was so hot and our work was gratis. We would have a group come in every Sunday to stay a week. It was just pines and humidity and the lake. I was a waterfront instructor—that meant that I was out on the pier from eight o'clock till dinner every day. Some of the little Scouts had never jumped into water before. And you know that in summer, by the time you had visited all your college friends for a couple weeks and had all your Coca-Cola parties, and by the time you had been at the beach for a couple of weeks, and by the time your college group had spent a week at Montreat, you were willing to go to Cheraw Beach and watch little girls who were afraid of the water. My big trip to the city every summer was to go to Richmond to visit my cousins."

I asked Waynette to tell me about her college days.

"I had a really good time at college, even though everything there was so strict. The school officials really did believe they were responsible for us. I lived a hundred miles from home, but I only went home overnight once from the time I went to college until the first Christmas vacation. For the first six months we couldn't spend a night off-campus, although we had one free weekend, and they counted Christmas for that weekend. We would actually go down to the bus station and take the eight A.M. express in the morning and be home by ten A.M. and then return to be back in the dormitory by nine that evening. As freshmen we could only date on two nights a week and we had to double-date with upperclasswomen in order to get permission to leave campus on a date. You can imagine how difficult it was to get an upperclass student to take you on a double date.

"Queens had about five hundred students then. I had just two roommates the whole four years. My freshman year I was with a girl who was nice and all but who had absolutely nothing in common with me. We were very poorly matched."

"Where would you go on a date?" I asked.

"A date was probably going to a movie. Sometimes the Charlotte day students at Queens would ask us to their homes. And the social scene at the other colleges nearby was so big. Davidson had socials, and of course the big weekend there was Homecoming. On Friday night of Home-coming there would be a senior formal, then the big game followed on Saturday, and then a formal dance that night with a big band. Then there were all the frat parties. Mid-winters: that was Davidson's big party time. In spring they had the Spring Follies or something like that.

"At Carolina they called those parties and dances the Spring Germans. At Queens we had a big May Day celebra-tion and a formal Christmas dance that was truly beautiful. And of course we had mixers at Queens to meet the David-son boys. Often the girls at Queens would get the Farlan-boro boys dates with their friends at Queens and the boys would get them dates with their friends at Davidson. The sororities and fraternities would often pair up for the parties. One time four of us even flew from Charlotte to Raleigh-Durham. We had just a weekend and we wanted to get there Friday night for the whatever it was.

"There was a special place on campus set aside just for May Day, the May Day Dell. The May Day festivities would begin with the election of the May Day queen and her maid of honor from the senior class. Each class would choose girls to be in the May Court. Then the queen and the court and the entire college would march down to the dell—we were all the queen's entourage. There would be a theme and all sorts of dances and songs. I was in the court one year. We just sat there with the queen looking pretty."

Waynette did not imitate how she had sat in the May queen's court, but she seemed scarcely able to keep from laughing. She shook her head in amusement.

"When I look back on it, I don't see how we got to do all those things with all the trouble in the economy back home and with the strictness at school. As sophomores we re-ceived more privileges. We got free weekends based on our grade average, so I worked hard. One time I got campused for three weeks. My roommate and I were supposed to double-date. We had to sign out together in the dean's office, but like everybody else, the couples would split off from each other outside the gates and arrange for a rendezvous time and place. Well, my roommate never showed up at the rendezvous. My date and I waited until fifteen past the hour, and when I went back to sign in the dean herself was on the desk that night. So that Monday night my roommate and I went before the student honor council and we both got campused for three weeks. The very next day my roommate had appendicitis and she went to the hospital and stayed there for the entire three weeks. All that time she got to have a ball at the hospital with visitors and all and I was stuck without even a roommate. I couldn't even visit her in the hospital and I couldn't have visitors myself."

"Why hadn't your roommate shown up at the rendezvous?"

"Her date's car had had a flat tire. When the dean asked me where Mary was, I said, 'I don't know!' and I didn't. Later on I was elected to the honor council and one of the things we used to do was conduct fire drills in the middle of the night. Those of us on the council knew when the drills would occur and so one night when we were going to have a drill I had my coat and stuff all ready and when the alarm woke us up Mary was so mad that I hadn't told her it was coming."

The events Waynette recounted were so vivid to her that her delight was evident. As Waynette related her stories she would occasionally break off in laughter or rub the moisture out of her eyes. She seemed to be acknowledging the folly of youth when she rolled her eyes and shook her head, but she also seemed to be reliving her past with considerable enthusiasm. She reached for her coffee cup and showed with an exasperated look that the coffee had grown cold.

"We could take swimming at Queens. Of course, we all had learned to swim in the millponds and river. But there was no pool at Queens so we got to go downtown to the YMCA two times a week for swimming classes. If you couldn't get a ride, you took a bus. That was in the Esther Williams days, and we put on a program that was really beautiful—*To Stella by Starlight*. We had white and black suits and sparkles on the caps we wore. Normally we had pastel bathing suits. We gave the program for our friends and parents of friends in town. My mother was so outdone with me that I hadn't told her to come and see the water ballet when she heard later from a friend how pretty it was.

"We couldn't wear socks uptown. Hose, heels, and hats— yes sir, we were representing our school. Clothes were expensive. Every Friday night we dressed up for dinner and then we had after-dinner coffee—this was in Sunday clothes and heels. We'd have a formal dinner before every concert. And then we had our horse-riding clothes for when we went riding out in the country. If you were caught drinking you'd be kicked out of school, and we had a very workable honor system for that and things like cheating. I worked on my tests like I had blinders on, because I knew I couldn't tell on anybody. There were supper clubs that we went to in the summer, but we weren't allowed to go to them during the school year. The clubs would have jazz bands and drinks. We couldn't keep a car until we started student teaching. I did my student teaching at Central High in Charlotte and it was the biggest building I had seen in my life. I was scared to death."

We sat in two formal chairs with white upholstery in the living room. On the walls hung portraits of the Clares' three children. They were hand-colored photographs and had been taken when each child was about four years old. The two pictures of the girls gave a sense of suspended animation, as if Catherine and Anne had both been about to say "Mama" or "I wanna go home," and in both pictures the girls' hands rested palms up in their laps. But the portrait of Alec was hard to look at without smiling, for it showed a towheaded, grinning elf. Alec's face was fixed with a determined look of devilish glee.

"Thinking back about Wayfare, it was a boom town back then and everyone thought that Wayfare was the up-and-coming place. I didn't know Archie well, but I knew he lived there. Although I didn't really know much of anything about it, we knew that some of the people who lived in Wayfare thought that they were aristocracy. There were some literary people who came from there and one family was related to one of the governors of the state. Wayfare was a real society-minded town. The ladies were all into the tea-party scene. I went out there a couple of times in high school. Archie's mother was really big into all that. She was a real club lady—garden club, home demonstration club, PTA. They put together cookbooks, had bazaars, put on men's suppers. Wayfare had a men's club, and if you were a man in Wayfare, you qualified."

Waynette stood up and drew the living-room curtains shut. "Do you know I can't even grow flowers in the garden? Every time I try to do something nice to the yard Archie mows it down." She said this with a smile, as if without question I too believed that Archie's insensitivity to flowers was both amusing and appalling. Archie used a lawnmower that looked like a miniature tractor, but for the last few weeks I had been the one who cut the grass. As far as I had been able to tell, the lawn had grown beyond the boundaries of the flower beds and extended well beneath the shrubbery along the sides of the house.

"Where we lived in Farlanboro was a nice section of town until I was seven, except for the cotton gin down the street. There were loads of children, a fire station nearby, lots of entertainment. During cotton season we'd play on cotton bales. We'd take shoeboxes and cut windows and glue tissue on them to make trains. I remember the ice man coming in a wagon pulled by a mule. We'd run behind it to get the drippings. We ordered ice by the pound in those days. There was a street that they blocked off every day for roller-skating.

"The boys worked then but the girls didn't. Bobby, my brother, worked with Grierson Seed in high school. He never has liked watermelon since. We did go to the beach some in summer. It's amazing where we swam, the mill-ponds. We did go out to a section of the Lumber River between Fulton and River Springs. Daddy would get off work and he'd take us over to the river for an hour in the afternoons. Daddy couldn't take any real vacations during the summer. He would work six days a week and then go to church on Sunday."

For the first time that evening the air-conditioning had switched off, and Waynette's voice now sounded loud in the comparative silence of the house. Waynette leaned back in her chair and began talking again in a softer voice.

"Not that Archie would hear us anyway," she said. "Rufus, one of my uncles, built me a playhouse when I was little. The biggest day of my life was when he brought it over and put it in the backyard and I had myself a log cabin. I remember one time when we were all worried because we had heard that Clay, another of my uncles, had gotten in a fight while he was at a hotel near Lake Waccamaw. That's the kind of thing you remember about being a child, the anticipation of good and bad things like Christmas or real bad storms.

"Mama was a real homemaker. She sewed, cooked, canned, and did all the domestic things you can imagine. She played bridge and she and Daddy were active in the Presbyterian church. She had her four sisters and her mother right there in Fulton just on the other side of the Campbell County line and she'd go there three times a week, at least. Those girls were all sufficient unto themselves—they were just very very close, all five of them. They would sit in Grandmama's house for hours and talk.

"We had blacks working for us in all sorts of capacities—cooks, gardeners, nannies, washerwomen. Every Monday Mama would take a huge pile of clothes with soap and starch and on Saturday we'd pick it up. The cook would have every other Sunday off and those Sundays Mama stayed home from church. No matter what age they were we called them by their first name. I remember Mama fussing at me because we had a colored girl come, Louise Adams. One Saturday I saw Mama and Miss Adams in the store and I yelled out, "Hey Mama! Hey Miss Adams!" I don't even remember why I hadn't called her Louise. I guess I was addressing her the way I would address any other adult. Later my mama said to me don't you call her Miss Adams. It was a patronizing sort of thing. Probably Miss Adams was as embarrassed as my mama was. There was no hostility, or at least none showed. The blacks deferred to us. But they always knew that if they needed help they could come to Daddy. Lots of Saturdays people—black and white—would come to the back door for help and money. Once one old white guy came to the front door. He was drunk.

"One summer I was riding the train to Richmond, and it was always real crowded. There was no segregation on those trains—this was in the forties—and there was an empty seat next to me and a colored woman sat in it. There was a soldier standing in front of us and he leaned across the colored woman and asked me didn't I want to sit next to him and I told him no thanks I was quite happy where I was. Before, the trains had always had black cars and white cars, and blacks always had to sit at the back of the bus. I can't really remember what happened to Indians back then. I don't remember much about them at all."

Waynette commented that there was class discrimination as well as racial discrimination in the society she knew growing up.

"Farlanboro was a rural place. And there were lots of little towns around that were even more isolated. Nice girls in Farlanboro—which meant for us any girl whose parents worried who their daughters hung around with—didn't associate with people in other communities, and the towns that were especially industrial had the reputation for being the roughest. There was a town down just across the South Carolina line—you don't need to know the name—that had lots of textile mills and there were times when the Farlanboro girls would gravitate toward that town or toward the boys who came from there. I was in junior high school and of course my friends and I found the boys from the rough towns appealing.

"There was this guy from the mill town, he had probably failed two years of high school already, and he was as tall as me and I found that interesting. I had always been taller than the boys my age. A fair came to Farlanboro and I went to it with some friends. My friend Deborah was quite forward and she knew I'd been eyeing this guy and just to spite me she went up and started talking to him. Well this guy from the mill town asked Deborah and me to ride the swings with him. There were two rows of swings that twirled you about. It was the next thing after the Ferris wheel. He was going to pay our way. I had no sooner gotten home than Mama said she knew who I rode the swings with and she was in an absolute disgrace—she was mortified. It was beyond her comprehension that I could be seen with him. Probably in the back of my mind I knew how mad she would be."

In the backyard Barney had started to bark, but Waynette seemed unconcerned. I was certain that everyone within a mile would be awakened. Waynette said that it was probably just a raccoon or opossum and that Barney would quit as soon as the animal ran away.

"One time in high school—it seems that for a while there we did nothing but drive around on the back roads—we were in a great wreck. There were six of us in a station wagon and four of our friends were in a car behind us. We would just go out onto the dirt and sand roads and the guys would see how fast they could go. We were on a sandy road and when we hit a patch of sand the wrong way we flipped over. A friend of mine, Jennifer, had long braids wrapped around her head and they fell down with the impact of the wreck and our friends in the car behind witnessed the whole thing. One of them kept saying, 'I saw Jennifer's long hair hanging out the window and I thought something horrible.' We were all fine and it was a miracle."

I had seen an old Polaroid snapshot taken of Waynette when she must have been sixteen or seventeen. She wore a scarf around her hair tied at the back of her neck, and she was sitting on a tree stump with her legs crossed. A mischievous glint shone in her eyes, and I could easily imagine her cutting up with her friends. I could see that Waynette had relished her life. One afternoon as Archie and I were heading out to the Lumber River to swim she stopped me to tell me about the time one summer when she was at the river with a bunch of her friends. She had been swimming with the others in deep water when all of a sudden her foot grazed a large rock on the bottom. She stood up on the rock and yelled out, "Hey, look everybody! I found me a rock to stand on!" But even as she spoke the rock moved out from under her and she and her friends suddenly realized that she had been standing on an alligator. In a panic they all raced for the shore. None of them saw or felt the alligator again that summer or any other.

"I don't know where to start about Essie, the children's nanny. When Cathy was little I had June working for me. June was a black woman who would have been in her twenties then, but she just wanted to work three days a week. Mama took care of Cathy on the other days. I don't know if Cathy knew which was her real home, because she spent so much time over at Mama's house. When little Alexander was born I would clearly need somebody who'd come every day, and the first day Essie came was the day before Alec was born. All my children were a week early. The plan was for Essie to start a week before Alec was due so she could get used to us and we could get used to her. She came and that night we went to the hospital and Alec was born. Essie came in and just sort of took over and she started tending to Alec right away. She seemed to know how to tend to babies very well, and she did everything. And then, when Alec was older, Anne was on the way and so Essie stayed. I thought, well, if I let Essie go, I won't do anything but stay around the house. And I could see my whole life of diapers and bottles and I knew that it wouldn't do. I had been teaching part-time, three classes a day, when Cathy was young. Then I decided to go back to school, so I went to Pembroke while Essie tended the children. I taught in River Springs, and then I moved to the elementary here in Farlanboro. I tell you, teaching sixth and seventh grades was something awful. Then at Farlanboro High, which at the time was the city school for whites, the French teacher was expecting, and I took her place. That was just a year before they began to build Lothian County High, which was to be integrated. When the county high school was completed I started teaching full-time again right here, beyond the fields that connect to our own backyard. That same fall that I began at the county high school, Mama died. In October.

"After Mama died we had Daddy here off and on. He loved to hunt bird and he would go hunting any time he could. And he loved baseball, the Legion ball games and all that when he was young. All the little towns around here had their teams and they'd play each other. In summer it was baseball and in winter it was birds. He was pretty sociable—had a lot of friends and they'd often have steak suppers or barbecues. Just men."

"What kind of social life did you and Archie have before the children were born?"

"Before we were married and for a little while after that Archie and I went dancing all the time. He never did play bridge, but then of course a lot of the things we did back then were involved with the church. The Queens stuff wasn't really high society, it was just the fifties culture. Nowadays it sounds like high society, but back then it was simply what was done. In the forties not many girls went down to the jazz dances that the blacks had, although Archie used to go and he would tell me about them. He heard some of the greatest musicians ever, right over in Fulton. The whites had to stay in the balcony and watch—they never were allowed to go down and dance or to mingle with the blacks.

"Archie was a drummer, you know, and he played for dances in Farlanboro and Lothian County. He was just in high school, but there were mostly older guys in the band. His band director in high school started up an independent band. They'd sit together at ball games and play, and they'd do programs for the school and the like. And then the director got together this little dance band and he himself played with them. Archie played percussion, one of his good friends played sax, and they had a pretty good little band."

Waynette announced that it was almost time for her to go to bed. I asked her to tell me about her children.

"I can't really begin to tell you about the children because we both know I will never stop once I get started. But you can ask them. They're all coming next weekend. But the other night when one of the kittens got into the house I was reminded of when the children were young and they'd let the kittens into the house to play. One night we put all the kittens back outside except for one that we couldn't find. Anne had the habit of getting up at night; she was always scared as a child. She would wake up and walk into our bedroom and crawl into bed with us. Well that night Anne and the kitten ran into each other in the hallway. They both screamed and the kitten disappeared until we finally found it behind the refrigerator. Anne kept waking up all the rest of that night with dreams of four little white paws coming at her. Anne was always scared. We'd all sit on the porch and tell ghost stories. She would start out, 'Now I'm going to tell a ghost story, but Mama, can I sit on your lap?' So to tell a ghost story she'd have to sit on my lap."

When I asked Waynette if she knew anything more about her ancestors, about the origins of her family in the Southeast, she confessed that she knew little about that. "My people were Cape Fear Scots," she said. "They came up the Cape Fear by boat from Wilmington, and they had to have come to Wilmington from Scotland. But why they came, I couldn't say. Unless it was for the land. There was a lot of good cheap land just waiting for them.

"Now I suppose it's time for bed. You know Archie. He'll be up knocking around at four in the morning as if he had something to do. He just makes coffee, wakes everybody up, and then he falls asleep on the couch."

Of course she was right. Archie would wake up and we would probably hear him making the coffee and opening the doors and windows at four in the morning. It occurred to me that Archie would probably always wake before dawn even when he no longer had work to do in the morning, even when he no longer had crops to raise. For Archie's mind moved to the rhythms of a world that only existed through his memory of it. One-man farming was already an anachronism, just like the tobacco culture and the Civil War. And in his telling of his family story, Archie familiarized the unfamiliar, giving detail and nuance to a conjecture, to an imagined version of the way things had been or might have been generations ago. Waynette's concentration on life as she had lived it conveyed all the delight of the everyday. Waynette had made a life out of joy in the growing, while Archie had made his life a study of growing and cutting, a study of appearances and disappearances, a study of the sleight of hand techniques that say, "Now you see it. Now you don't."

EIGHT

IT WAS ON a hot day at the bleak end of July, a day fit for nothing but the river, that Archie told me his dream. In the dream, after driving the eleven miles to the Sinclair farm, Archie found that someone, in a fit of high comedy and bitter satire, had pasted greenbacks to his corn. Crisp green rectangles dangled from the leaves and the tips of corn spears and fluttered with the illusion of movement, row upon row, *novus ordo seclorum, e pluribus unum*. The entire field appeared as a single fabric undulating in the early morning heat. As he approached they seemed to multiply, and he heard the rigid edges of the bills scrape across one another like blades.

He didn't have to muse upon the language of images in order to decode his dream. For all the effort he had put into his crops, he might as well have thrown a bale of cash into a field and waited to see what was left come August. And he might as well have spent his time pasting dollar bills to reedy leaves of cane as disk and sow and cultivate and all the rest. He ploughed borrowed cash into a field and carried away a perishable permutation of greenback. The crop was only a distinctive place and form in which to store the bank's money. He gained no interest on it, but he lost his time and labor and the blood of his little finger to the blade. He offered up his bulk barn and traded on his disk. Borrow come spring, pay come fall, winter, spring, and summer. Borrow and pay, pay, pay. Again. Always. Pay. And then some. And more. A field is a place where something is always dying, even when a crop lifts itself up green and shining in the gray light of earth. A field is just a place to store money for a season. A field is a deferment, a way of shifting a humanly created form of highly organized energy into the service of an extraordinarily intricate system of waste. And after a season a field has been changed by the farmer the way a dollar bill has been changed by the fingers that handled it: a few different creases and wrinkles mark its face and some of its green has been scraped away by the brains and muscles that worked it.

Nature loves a spendthrift. Archie saw this in all the little Washingtons, Lincolns, and Hamiltons that fluttered in the morning breeze of his dream. A field is a place where resource dwindles. *Out of many, one,* seemed a formula and statement of his economic policy. For the logical extension of borrow and pay more later would be to borrow many and return one. *E pluribus unum.* Row after row swayed to the incantation. And then the acrid smell in the air began to make sense, for Archie could see that the green crop was burning, row upon row of green patriots vanishing into a dim haze. Someone had torched his field, and before his eyes the crop was turned to air and ash.

/ / / / /

Archie had experienced similar moments before, moments of foreboding, doubt, despair, or whatever best describes that wide-eyed amazement, disbelief, and finally scorn that he felt as he watched himself dispense money and effort in the face of certain failure. They had occurred in 1979, 1983, and during bad spells in other years, these moments when the fields had appeared to be papered with money, when the rising wind and the glimpse of a flame meant that the inevitable would follow. Only, unlike this summer, those years he had been able to brush off the grim news, even when it had led him into debt. One year it had been too much sun. Another it had been too much rain. Another it had been pests. And one year it was the CIA.

"I didn't find out until years later that the CIA did it. This was in 1968, I believe, somewhere in there. They tried to drown out the Cuban sugarcane and tobacco crops. What it amounted to was they wanted to cause an agricultural disaster in Cuba by seeding iodide crystals in the sky. We had a high-pressure area over North Carolina at the time. When we have high pressure over the Piedmont, which happens in July usually, it causes a south-southwest flow of air, and that summer the high pressure brought all the humid air and the iodide crystals up here. We had rain for three solid months. The ground never dried out enough to cultivate. We planted and that was it. I lost sixteen thousand dollars that year. That year I had fifty acres of cotton and I didn't get to pick it. There was no disaster relief then. As a result of that year I had a double allotment of tobacco the next year and I made all of that. We had four families living on the property that next year and I gave each of them a tobacco crop to take care of. I was lucky to have people who wanted it on a share basis, and, even though the rain gave me fits, I came out of that debt real quick the next year on tobacco alone.

"The Glencairn farm was in a soil-bank program of the sixties. The government paid you to leave the land idle. It's sad to say, but the most consistent success I've had with that farm has come from leaving it idle. The land at that farm was left idle for ten years. That was due to a policy to decrease surpluses in a period of enormous surpluses. The government didn't know what to do with such an incredible stockpile. They even subsidized the building of silos—throughout the country there are acres of concrete silos constructed in this period. Kansas is still full of them, all the states in the Corn Belt are. Then Nixon came in in seventy-two and sold every bit of the stuff to anybody who wanted to buy it—Russia, China, Eastern Europe. Until then we had restrictions. We couldn't sell it directly to Eastern Europe, since the Soviet Union wanted a hand in it first. Nixon sure got the economy to rolling again with both hands and feet. And he devalued the dollar—cut it in half. Beans went from two twenty-five to six dollars, even to nine dollars. There was a tremendous demand for corn, which rose from one dollar to two-fifty and topped out at three dollars. That's when agriculture kicked into gear, the early seventies, and land prices rose, and eventually real estate taxes, too.

"But that storm boiled all summer. You might see sunrise. Might not. We got an inch a day sometimes there for a week stretch. Damn, for two weeks at a time. It rained continually. That summer I believe we got like fifty inches of rain when that's above normal for twelve months. I may be exaggerating, but it was a hell of a lot of rain. I'll put it this way—the soil got saturated in the spring and never dried out until the equinox, in the fall.

"At that time not many knew what the CIA was. It was secret. Then I believe it was mainly an army intelligence operation and later it was transferred to the State Department. We didn't hear about the Cuban sugarcane crop disaster as such until the seventies, where things had loosened up to the point where the country was beginning to get some derogatory political propaganda about the CIA. People began not to like what the CIA was up to. Papers and magazines started looking for things about the organization that people would like to hear and they began to harass the CIA. Well it came out that the CIA had flown this mission in the Caribbean and it had such an adverse effect on the Southeast that they developed a policy saying it was too risky to try to destroy our enemies' crops. It did have an effect on Cuba, but not as much as on our own Southeast, from Jacksonville to Richmond. 'Too much rain' was the expression. And it was, too."

/ / / / /

All human intention erodes under corrosive time and capricious weather. The farmer counts off on his fingers responses to failure as if they were workers he would call to help barn the tobacco. One: There's always next year, which *has* to be better than this. Two: The government *must* do a better job of stabilizing the agricultural economy. Three: The damn chemical and machine producers, the damn greedy banks have caused this. Four: It is the way of the South, the way of land to be dispersed and the people to scatter, the way of families to lose the land as they search for other meanings in other places. Five: It is blind necessity and there is nothing to be done about it. Six: This is the vale of soul making, after all. Seven: Who cares? Eight: Damn it all anyway.

So the government's rain fell on the land of Archie Clare and on the farms of thousands of other people like him. A few seasons later it would be drought. The year after that it would be a fine crop but a flooded market. And then pests. And then drought again, or rain.

A poet once said that every man is the seed of a ghost. Archie Clare has begun to believe that he has come into his own full-grown identity prematurely. For, as he sees it, in the weathers of the sky, the economy, the field and leaves, there is no shade that will shelter him, scarcely any air that he can breathe.

The kernel of wheat. The fathom of corn. Seeds are bodies in transit, the shadows of weeds, and trees, and people that once lived and now are gone but that, through the sheer extravagance of things, will live again. In the insanity of the far-flung business of American farming, the seeding of clouds and the cultivation of tons of water, this broadcast engendering the earth and sky both, what could possibly make sense? And even though Archie Clare understands the senselessness of his actions, he seems to be stuck. Stuck in—what should he call it? A ritual? A habit? An addiction? A fate? A passion? Only a seed dressed in shirt, pants, and boots would continue under such circumstances to drag his body and his tools and his crops across the face of the earth.

/ / / / /

Archie and I had climbed into the El Camino once again. We were headed north on one of the nameless back roads that stretched through the drought that summer. Archie had brought along a newspaper clipping dated March 11, 1958, ten years or so before the CIA rains, a day when a small earthquake had shaken Farlanboro. As Archie drove, I read the article. The event had taken place during the time of planting. Farlanboro had found out that the earthquake had been caused by an atomic bomb that fell out of a U.S. Air Force B-47 from fifteen thousand feet onto a small farming town called Mars Bluff, about fifty miles away. According to the Pentagon the bomb was unarmed, which must mean that it didn't have the components necessary to create an explosion through atomic fission. But when the bomb hit the ground the triggering mechanism blew up with the force of five thousand pounds of TNT. The blast completely destroyed one house and damaged five others and a church. Children, playing in the yard when the bomb fell, survived the blast uninjured, and a woman who was sewing inside the house had time to run out the door before the house collapsed.

/ / / / /

Earlier that morning Waynette had told me the story of Spaghetti. For her daughters, Cathy and Anne, Spaghetti was part of the routine of growing up. Cathy and Anne were members of a group of little girls. They would begin their afternoon play by gathering up the group, going from one house to another, calling out for Evelyn and Lizzie and Laura. Once they had gathered, they would never begin the serious business of play until they had made their pilgrimage halfway around the block to the garage of the Farlanboro Funeral Home on Chapel Street. Walking into the open garage, the girls would sneak up to a long narrow box that leaned upright against one of the walls. All giggling and nudging would stop at that point and no one would need to hush the others. A couple of the girls would put their hands in their pockets. One would look back at daylight outside the garage door. One would open the front of the box. They would all look inside at a shriveled body, naked except for a loincloth, with olive-brown skin and a gash—sewn up by the mortician—that ran vertically from the center of his forehead back to the middle of his skull. *Spaghetti* was the only Italian word anyone in Farlanboro knew. And so that became his name. Spaghetti had come to town with the circus in the twenties or thirties—no one was really certain when—and someone killed him with a tent spike. No one claimed the body or officially identified it. He was embalmed and remained out of the ground, waiting for a name and a place. Some Italian residents of the town took up a collection and finally buried him about ten years ago. There were other peculiar things in the funeral home garage, like the bodies of stillborn babies in jars. But it was Spaghetti the little girls went to see. The only mummy around. The girls, grown up, remember that they were always scared when they went to see him, but that he never became the subject of ghost stories. When I asked if they ever touched the body, she said that they couldn't remember touching it, that, in fact, the body might have rested in its coffin underneath a sheet of glass.

/ / / / /

In a world that welcomes drought over downpour, what can the sky send that a farmer can hold on to? Is there any final value in weather when profit margins explode after a drought? From the perspective of the hawk, the farmer's activity appears as diurnal ramblings across a plain. Archie's path traces the sketchy wanderings within an electron cloud: anyone interested in locating him would face the uncertainty of knowing that Archie was somewhere within a certain area, that he could be found at one of a limited number of points on the roads and sites situated on his circuit, but not knowing precisely which. Over the days and weeks Archie's movements draw a series of interconnected loops that radiate from Farlanboro like the edges of an aster's petals or the imperfect lines that a child with a compass draws to create a star or bracelet or crown. From the hawk's perspective these loops may have their interest or even their beauty, but for the farmer the important motions are those that involve exchanges of power. Archie covers a lot of ground. The mileage that he accumulates is one index to the work he accomplishes and to the avidity with which he pursues his business. Always on the move, Archie carries the miles on his back, in his step, and in his laugh. But, however much he moves laterally upon the flat earth, he recognizes that vertical motions are, when all is said and done, the ones that matter most. Rising and falling have far greater symbolic and practical significance than migration. All the movements on the circuit shift matter and energy from one place to another. But burials and resurrections are what make the farmer's day. Rain gotta fall. Seed gotta grow. Up. Down. All other motions are efforts to prepare, to coax, to forestall, to make sure that all the right things are in all the right places when the sky falls.

Archie seems to be in the business of tracing lines along the various highways that run from place to place in his world. But the lines that matter are the ones he scratches in the soil to catch whatever falls from the sky. And what comes from the sky has everything to do with seeds rising up to blink in downy light, with the green matter of leaves thickening and ripening. The orbits Archie draws by his meanderings to and from Farlanboro, the widespread places he visits in order to do his work—these, like any series of snapshots that might be taken from the El Camino as it shudders down a road, are images that combine to form the same old picture of what Archie knows. Fields and roads and houses will stick around, for the most part. It's the green and yellow and white and brown stuff that flourishes for a while before it's mown down, that's the news. And it always seems that a particular crop is here and gone before he knows it.

/ / / / /

As we headed north toward the river, we approached a huge column of smoke. The entire sky east of Wayfare was filled with the commotion of a field being hauled bodily into the sky. As a circle of flame moved from the edges to the center of the field, smoke rose like a thunderhead, like a great hand shielding eyes against the sun. When the circle of fire reached a certain point of tightness it imploded and seemed to vault huge fragments of field into the sky, a sublimation of field scrap and grain litter into the dark tumult of air. Even as we passed the burning field the smoke became gray and, like the spume of cold breath disintegrating into a thousand wisps of steam, gradually disappeared. Archie observed that there was really no reason to burn a field this time of year—he couldn't make sense of it. It occurred to me that maybe someone had had enough of drought.

Soon we turned right in the middle of Wayfare and approached Riverbank, the public beach on the Lumber River just a mile beyond the town. Archie had wanted to take a canoe down the river, and he had arranged for Waynette to pick us up at a river bend three miles downstream. Riverbank was where Archie had swum as a child, and it had remained the most popular swimming site for most of the families in Lothian County. A broad pool had formed along a gently sloping bank, and the languid current had deposited lots of fine sediment and sand there. Riverbank was private property and at various times had been closed to the public, handed over to the county for administration as a park, and abandoned by landowner and all authorities alike. People had taken to driving their cars and trucks all the way down to Riverbank over the most prodigious network of ruts and tree roots imaginable.

For the past few years Riverbank had enjoyed a reputation for being a rough place, and Archie referred to the people who went there to swim with their car doors open and stereos blasting as "the crowd." When we arrived around noon the crowd was boisterous and the noise from the cars and trucks bounced through the woods. We loaded a Thermos of drinking water, a bag of apples, some cushions, and two paddles into the canoe, climbed in, and soon left the booming cars and squealing children behind. Archie had looped his waterproof camera around his neck. Barney ran along the bank until the roots and fallen trees grew thick and hampered his maneuvering, and then he took off into the woods.

The woods were dark and they looked, well, stupid. Pointless. Senseless. Too dense. Too hot. Full of poison ivy and bugs. The roots and knees of the trees were gray. It seemed that every leaf was laden with dust. A group of turkey vultures appeared above the river. They too looked foolish, teetering in the still air, bony codgers wearing feathers. Occasionally one would light on a branch and stare into space with the cold glare of an auditor. Six, nine, a dozen rose above the trees. They came so close we could see their red heads, their gray undersides. Half gray, half black, they seemed to chase us down the winding river as if to deliver us from evil, from the infamy of our flesh. The river turned and the feathered cloud ascended out of our minds to waver out of sight in the sky.

We had been on the river scarcely an hour. The flow remained sluggish and the water was low, lower than Archie had ever seen it. A couple times we came to fallen trees that spanned the channel. We would rake our paddles against the tree or climb out and straddle it as we lugged the canoe over. The river began to double back on itself and undertake a series of serpentine maneuvers through the woods. And then, for the first time all day, we heard the sound of rushing water.

White water was unheard of on the deep Lumber River, with its sandy and muddy banks. The only rocks in its bed were gravel size. When we turned another bend we saw that the channel narrowed and appeared to end in a wall of roots at the base of a huge cypress. The canoe butted up against the roots and we scrambled out. The roots formed a tangled matrix that filtered the river into a short, three-foot waterfall. Downriver the channel was only six feet wide for twenty yards, and we could see that as the river widened it also dropped a few feet over the next hundred yards, creating a rapid current. Getting into the canoe and sending it

on its way would be tricky because of the drop and the current. We shoved the canoe and jumped in. That was that.
We sped downstream, the canoe grazed the shore, and we
lightly brushed the bushes that overhung the river. I shud-
dered without knowing why as I sensed something drop
into the boat. What falls out of the sky into a boat on a low
river in the middle of the worst drought in memory?

"There's a snake in the boat!" I yelled and flung myself
into the river. The snake had fallen through my lap right
between my bare feet into the bottom of the boat. The only
way to get rid of the snake would be to scrape it up my legs
with the paddle. I hit the river, cursing, faster than I could
think.

"What?" Archie was laughing. "Are you joking around?"

"There's a snake in the boat!"

He too hit the water.

It has become his favorite story about me. "I didn't know
that boy could curse like that," he remembers as he chuck-
les. Chest deep in the river I saw a snake in every root and
leaf and branch. We stood as Archie laughed. Archie had
tried to hold his camera above water when he jumped. We
pulled the boat back to the cypress roots and the snake
slithered in the bow.

"Damn if that isn't a water moccasin. Big, too."

"Let's throw it out and get back in the boat."

"Let me take a picture of it first." We stood in the dismal
water slipping off cypress roots and took pictures of the
snake. Five photographs later Archie flipped the snake out
of the canoe with his paddle. We found that we had to
move closer to shore in order to empty the canoe. We pulled
it through the water until we were thigh deep in treachery.
We knew for a fact that there was at least one snake in the
water, for we had dumped it there. Not that way, we both
seemed to say as we tipped the canoe over upstream. It was

too late—we'd filled it with water. After a few moments of coordinated effort we fished the canoe out, slurried the water back into the river, and climbed in.

"You sure can cuss. Never would have known it."

I eyed the trees and saw in every vine a loathsome coil.

A man suspended behind glass until his flesh and bones assume the hard polished shine of molasses. A thunderhead towering overhead like a mountain and revealing the immensity of the sky. Smoke rising. A snake falling into a boat. Sometimes it takes the thrill of adrenaline and reflexive action to remind us that meaning lies somewhere other than in language and symbols. It takes having a snake drop onto your lap to appreciate that knowledge can be simply a matter of sensations. Sometimes all the ingredients necessary for a symbolic order are present and they even appear to dovetail neatly into one another, yet they still don't add up.

When I was a young boy I had a recurring and vivid dream that imitated the credit sequence of a popular weekly TV cartoon. In the cartoon a character fell from the sky into a field and after a few seconds of rain and sun, sprouted up with cornstalks and sunflowers. I suppose that this was an image of the resolution achieved by all cartoon worlds where the hero—or heroine—always bounces back no matter how many times he is pummeled and squashed by his opponents. In my dream I was the one who fell and who, after a spell of muffled darkness giving way to a vague, amniotic glow, experienced my own germination in unwinding ascent through the soil to the realization that where my head should be was instead the entire blue sky.

Even though Archie Clare did not hear the voice of the whirlwind when he stood in his field, and even though he did not see in drought a moral judgment upon his actions, the peculiar coincidence of labor, drought, and debt that stole upon him in the summer of 1986 had all of the familiarity of both fate and choice about it.

One afternoon that summer Archie walked out to the front porch and picked up the *Farlanboro Exchange*. On the front page he read a story about a farmer who had been clearing some wooded land for cultivation somewhere in Lothian County. The farmer had removed the roots, large stones, and other debris and had disked the ground deeply. As he stood beside his tractor, he lit a cigarette, kicked the dirt from his heels, tugged on the brim of his hat, and watched a man fall, spread-eagle, from the sky. The farmer hadn't noticed the airplane that had flown by overhead and dropped the man. The farmer watched as the man from the sky disappeared into the ground. Thirty seconds later the man stood up, brushed off his pants and shirt, and walked away.

///////

NINE

WHEN THEY CAME home on the first weekend in August, the Clare children told me their favorite story about their father. When Archie was a boy of three or four, he was scared to sleep in his own bed. When he crawled into bed with his mother and father they assumed that he was going through a phase during which he was simply afraid of the dark. But as Archie's fears persisted they investigated further and finally they got him to show them what had been scaring him so. He pointed to the window in his bedroom that opened out onto the porch. Looking through the window his parents realized that they had been blind to the obvious. What they saw was a large peach crate; from between the gray ribs of its boards gleamed flashes of white.

As the Clare children tell it, their father's childhood nightmares began when Archie's father and someone who was helping him on the farm were digging a well on the Clare property. The Clares had always heard that a Union soldier had supposedly died on the property and been buried there instead of in the nearby cemetery that had been set aside for blacks and Union soldiers. While digging the well, John Leonade Clare discovered and dug up a skeleton that everyone believed to be the soldier's. He had intended to move them to the cemetery, but somehow the bones, which had been burnished clean by time, had lost their priority and ended up in a peach crate on the back porch.

Another version of the story has the bones unearthed by the people who lived on the Clare land before Archie's grandfather, James Leonade Clare, bought it. A woman who hated the Union made her sons dig up the bones of the dead Union soldier after her husband, who had buried the soldier on the property, died. She didn't want Union bones on her land.

When Archie pointed through the window of his room it was toward the skeleton in the peach crate. His parents moved the skeleton to a shed where it rested until neighbors started complaining of thieves stealing from their grain bin. The Clares had the neighbors put the skeleton in the grain bin, and the neighbors never had a problem with thieves again. Years later, when Archie was in high school, the Clares gave the skeleton to one of the young men from Wayfare who was going off to the university to study to become a doctor.

/////

By the time the Clare children had assembled at their parents' home in the second week of August, the drought had changed the world of Archie and Waynette Clare, of Auntie Jess and Dan L. and their family, for good. The border-belt tobacco markets had opened, but nobody was selling tobacco. In a normal year Archie would have started cropping and barning tobacco in mid-July, but here it was August and he had not yet barned any of his crop. What farmers had been saying for months might still be true: tobacco will wait for rain. But the tobacco in Archie's fields had begun to look like not even rain would do it any good. Archie had gone ahead and topped the tobacco, removing the flowers at the tip of the tobacco stalk in late June, and had applied sucker control, a chemical that prevented the growth of new shoots from the joints of leaf stems. These procedures directed all of the plants' energies into the production of tobacco leaves.

Archie had already seen his field of cantaloupe and watermelon, planted to fetch pocket money for cigarettes and gasoline, waste away. He had found six tolerable watermelons in two acres. A funk had settled over Auntie Jess and Sudi Jane, who missed the influx of cash that they, Dan L., Jeeter, and Cooter Tom would normally have received for produce and tobacco harvesting. Without the diversion of working with the tobacco crop, Jeeter had begun ranging farther from home with his friends from the cities in the North. One afternoon as Archie and I drove south toward the tobacco market we drove past Auntie Jess's house and I saw that the basketball hoop had entirely disappeared from the goal. A litter of puppies frisked and panted under the willow oak, and a cluster of plastic flowers, bright red, flashed in sunlight through a window.

Archie's digestion had troubled him all summer, and he had tried several ways to improve it. He had abstained from whiskey, and for a while that seemed to help. Then he started with the Jim Beam again, and he convinced himself that that helped, too. He mentioned quitting smoking but seemed to dismiss that option with the very next breath. It was becoming clear that, however discreetly she expressed her annoyance, Waynette was growing more and more impatient with Archie hanging around the house. He had never before spent so much time at home during the summer, and Waynette was almost looking forward to the beginning of the school year.

The kittens had been moved out to the woodshed, which Archie, who rarely applied his handiwork around the house, had reconstructed, replacing the rotting plywood and posts. The blueberry bushes that Archie had transplanted into his yard the year before were producing sweet, fat berries thanks to the persistent heat and daily watering with the garden hose. On the back porch various baskets held butter beans, field peas, and tomatoes: two small watermelons sat in the corner. The pungent smell of overripe cantaloupe filled the air. The produce, purchased at produce stands stocking fruit and vegetables grown out of state, almost made people forget the drought. The Clares had been eating their own Silver Queen corn for the last two weeks, but the supply was dwindling. Most of the ears had abnormally small and blistered kernels that were, nonetheless, sweet. Some of the ears had irregular-size kernels in broken rows. We cut off the tapered ends of the ears where the kernels had not grown. An immediate concern was making sure that there would be enough corn and produce to provide the children with a conventional summertime meal at the Clares'. So July dragged itself along into August, the crops seemed dead in fields, and the Clares continued to endure the routine heat. At the end of July, almost as if in defiance of the drought, the crepe myrtles continued to lift themselves into blossom.

And then, on the first Thursday in August, the sky over Lothian County grew dark, at first with a dull, uneven gray, and then with a blustery blue-black cloud that was so low and so large that from no vantage in Farlanboro could the top of the storm be seen as it stretched over fifty thousand feet above. Quite unbelievably and quite casually, the sky opened up, and it rained. Despite the size of the storm cloud, only certain portions of Lothian County received the downpour. And by the time Archie visited the tobacco in Campbell County later that afternoon, all of the water had been absorbed into the soil. Normally after a good rain the water puddled between the rows for twenty-four hours or more. But the ground was parched and the rainwater disappeared as it fell. It wouldn't be enough rain to save the soybeans and the corn, but it might do for the tobacco. It gave Archie, at least, that hope.

The rain seemed to lift Archie's spirits just in time for the return of the children. He would wait to harvest the tobacco since, now that it had received some rain, it would soon start to fill out. But as Archie continued his visits to the crops, he became more and more dismissive of any topic having to do with farming. He made light of the drought and the rain alike by saying that farmers always had had it rough and farmers usually believed that they had it rougher than they actually did. Maybe thinking of the children reminded him of the generally understood purpose of farming, which was, after all, to provide food and a living. The impending return of the children somehow underscored for Archie the certainty that a way of life was coming to an end. Now they would always be only visitors. If he and Waynette could hold on to their land they would pass it down to the children, of course. But neither had any illusions about the children returning for good to live and raise families in Lothian County. As the years of his life accumulated and came home to him in the forms of his grown children, Archie seemed to develop a great distaste for the inconsequential successes and failures of the season.

/////

Catherine McKay Clare, Robert Alexander Clare, and Anne Leonade Clare were born to Waynette and Archie in 1958, 1961, and 1963, respectively. Cathy had become an English teacher, Alec a carpenter, and Anne, with a degree in art history, worked in a department of the National Gallery in Washington, D.C.

It was ninety degrees at eleven o'clock on a Saturday morning and Cathy, Alec, and Anne seemed immune to the heat. Cathy and Anne headed down the street to go for a walk, and Barney followed. Alec sat in a lawn chair in the shade of the large oak in the backyard and scooped up a bunch of gum balls from the ground. He threw them one by one at the kittens hiding behind a patch of spearmint that grew alongside the back porch. I asked Alec if he had ever intended to farm with his father.

"My very first memory is of shaking a tree in the woods. I got left in the truck down somewhere between Auntie Jess's and the swamp, and that's where they found me, holding on to a gray sapling in the woods. It was someplace where Daddy was farming. If you can call that helping, that was the beginning of my working a farm, I guess. I did have it in my head that I'd be a farmer somewhere someday, but through the years when I was growing up somehow the idea that farming couldn't cut it, that farming just couldn't give a person a decent living—well, that idea was just about in everything you do and see when you hang around the farm. In all the little stuff that goes on you can see that farming just doesn't form a complete picture, if you know what I mean.

"Most of the things I remember about when I was a kid are picture-induced. I spent a lot of time at the Bethanys', the black family that lived down in Campbell County on the land where Daddy's bulk barns are, the Glencairn place. From the time I was two until I was eight years old I spent most of my time with them doing their kind of stuff. Chasing chickens and whatnot. I spent a lot of time there, I sure did. Me and Buster Bethany were the same age, but we never did go to school together or anything—you know how that goes. Childhood is just mud, dirt, and chickens. The Bethanys' was where I first smelled stuff like wood-burning stoves, fresh-ploughed dirt, and so on. Essie, our nanny, would rate up there with my early memories, but that was about thirteen years' worth.

"One time Daddy set off a Roman candle and a bottle rocket and I saw the rocket take off and I thought Daddy'd gone to the moon. Mama had taken me back inside, and I cried like hell even though everybody was telling me that Daddy was fine. It wasn't the Fourth of July, and that may be why it was so strange to me. Wooah, did you see that?" He had thrown a gum ball toward a kitten that had ventured out onto the grass and the kitten had flipped backward when the gum ball bounced over its head.

Alec Clare was a good-humored, fair-haired, blue-eyed man who often wore a CAT cap on his head of long hair, which was drawn back into a ponytail. The sharp brow and deep-set eyes of his father were unmistakable. Most of his approach to life and work seemed to be summed up in the beer he held in his hand at noon and the rock music he loved. He had a dog named Thomas Wolfe, but it is doubtful that Alec has ever finished a novel by his dog's namesake. Like his mother, Alec had had a good time at college, but unlike her he attended three different universities, never graduated, and never enjoyed a great deal of success at any of them. Alec's intelligence was oriented toward people and toward the land. He showed a genuine interest in the things he studied, and he was clearly capable of excellent work, but he wouldn't apply himself to book learning and so barely passed his classes, when he passed at all. As he proceeded through his coursework he gradually began to focus on forestry and woodworking. He delighted in pointing out whatever stage of development a particular field or pond exhibited, and he would run through the sequences of events that would shape the pond or field over the years.

Alec and Archie got along reasonably well, although I gathered that there had been undercurrents of the usual conflicts between father and son. Alec's appearance alone represented values and a way of life that Archie found foreign. Ironically, Alec's sweeping mustache made him the spitting image of James Leonade Clare. But Alec had an attitude toward life that was much more relaxed than James's would have been. He had moved to Raleigh when a contractor he knew offered him work pounding nails. He grew interested in carpentry and began to study in order to apply for a contractor's license. What Archie disapproved of in his son seemed to be his lightheartedness. Alec worked hard, but he just didn't seem to approach anything with a great deal of seriousness.

"As far as working on the farm goes, I was probably put to doing something pretty early, but most of the time when I went with Daddy down to the farms it was playing, dog-chasing, wide-open kid play. You know, whatever you can get away with under the eyes of a woman who's looking after seven kids at the same time, or while you're with a farmer off doing something and leaving a kid to himself on the edge of a field. As I grew up I suppose that I became a wrench hander and a nut twister for a long time. When I was fourteen I could do most anything with the David Bradley tractor—no, that was at twelve years or so. But anyway, I drove a tractor for Daddy through high school, especially in the melon fields. I guess my first paying job was working produce or cropping tobacco. I did make money on a cucumber patch when I was thirteen. That was with Cathy, and that was when I bought my savings bonds."

Alec was quite reflective as he talked. Sometimes a puzzled look came over his face when he seemed to find that he had less to say on a topic than he had imagined. I asked him about how he learned to use the farm equipment.

"How do you learn how to work a tractor? Well, you start with a lot of riding first, and then you move on to cultivation and planting and moving things. I remember one time I got on the tractor and cranked it up—this is one of them David Bradleys—anyway, Daddy was parked behind one of the old tobacco barns with his pickup truck. Well, all I had to do was to put it in gear and the tractor took a right and I nailed the rear end of Daddy's truck. I had hit the throttle first and then the gear. The tractor's front end flew up and I scrambled around, poking everything on the dashboard. It's like there's an entire farm in front of me and I crank the tractor up and immediately rear-end my daddy's truck.

"That was some tractor ride. But Daddy did the same thing once himself. Boy, I remember the time he came home after he'd done it. He had an old green pickup, and he pulled the tractor into the truck—it just rolled right into it and buckled the truck in two. When he came home that night, well, there was a little redemption there. It's some kind of life: the higher it falls in from, the better it feels."

Alec grinned and wanted to make sure I appreciated his point. He brushed his legs almost continually and said that he was prone to bug bites. Apparently, mosquitoes considered him a great delicacy.

"Cutting firewood, I guess, was my first introduction to treeing. I remember once I went with Daddy down into Campbell County and it was the first time I'd seen a belligerent drunk. There was a ditch bank that Daddy would clean for a woman whose husband had died. He pulled in there one afternoon to say hello and before he even got out of the truck he said, 'Lord, she's drunk.' There was a man living with her and he had only one leg. Well, the woman ran out onto the porch and down the steps and this guy comes into the doorway with a gun like I had never seen before and he starts shooting at her feet to get her to come back into the house. It's just plain rough down there."

"What about Wayfare and your Uncle John's—did you go over there much when you were young?"

"Wayfare—I did a lot of growing up over there. We'd go over there once a week. As far as I remember we never did much work over in Wayfare, although we did some combining over there. Uncle John had cows, pigs—always had something going on over there. He had a fishing pond over there and hunting, too. Uncle John lived in the Sandhills, and that was a different kind of woods. John used to have a big campout during hunting season, like one of the big hunts, like something out of the Black Forest in Germany or in the mountains of Wyoming. We went way up in the Sandhills and it seemed like everything up there was theirs, like the property went on forever. The boys would hunt quail and the men would hunt deer. I never was much of a duck hunter, getting up at five in the morning to freeze your ass off for hours in the middle of a swamp and to see two ducks nine thousand miles above you."

Alec picked up one of the kittens and held it in his lap. The kitten gnawed on Alec's hand and flexed its paws against his arm.

"Oh, there's lots about the life associated with farming that you can't beat, and occasionally flashes of those hunting trips will come to me, things like playing in a ditch with tadpoles and the dog there and Buster Bethany and cornstalks withering away but still standing. But as often as not it's getting yelled at that I remember, like the time I bent up a disk tongue, and that was a lot of money.

"And I remember burning fields. Usually it was small grains and soy we burned. One time up on Uncle Billy's land in the Sandhills we were burning a field that had already been combined. We'd soak a burlap bag with gasoline, light it up, and drag it from behind a truck on an eight-foot line. Being a kid, I was driving all over the place, not in a circle like I was supposed to. I think what happened was I stopped to get my bearings because there were smoke and flames everywhere and I couldn't see. So when I started up the truck I was too anxious and spun the wheels and started to get stuck. I finally calmed down and rocked the truck out of the ruts and I just barely got out of there. I came home with singes all over my face.

"Yeah, for a little while I used to say to myself, sure, I might farm. I like the idea of farming land and working it, but I guess that I had given up on the idea by junior high school. I had come to realize that it wasn't worthwhile. Hell, at that point my dad was into debt—how is he going to truthfully tell somebody he should get into farming with that kind of trouble hanging over him? All along as I was growing up it was pretty obvious that farming wasn't going to last."

"But what about the place, what about the land and Lothian County? Do you miss it? Do you ever think of moving back?"

"The land is too flat. Down in the swamp would be the only place I'd find interesting enough. Or up in the Sandhills. I guess all along I thought that being a farmer would be it, would be what I'd be if I stuck around in Lothian County. You take farming out of the picture and you don't have anything left down here. There's no work to speak of, at least none that interests me. And it must have been understood as I was growing up that I wouldn't get into farming. The thing to do would have been to acquire more land if the plan had been for me to farm. But we never did.

"The old man has thought I was crazy many times before, but when Julie, my wife, and I bought twenty acres up north of Durham he really thought we were crazy. He thinks we shouldn't a bought that twenty acres. I suppose in a way we're still farmers. I came home one day a few weeks ago and I was really steamed. 'That's why I don't want to be a farmer,' I was saying. I'd broken a sickle blade on the neighbor's mower and I'd been looking at it all damn day. I had been mowing a horse pasture full of hay and I hit a stump. But you could say that we're dabbling in farming—we want to garden and we do it all organic. I mean, why do we want twenty acres? That's a damn big yard. The old man's right—it *is* crazy. But as for going back home and living, naw. You'll always have three kinds of people living in these counties—Indians, blacks, and whites—and you'll always have problems associated with that. People down here are too prejudiced and too slow to change. I saw enough of people fighting over stupid things in high school.

"One time when I was a boy," Alec said, "I was painting a fence red down at the farm off the highway and I turned the paint can over on myself. I mean I put enough paint on me to kill myself. I'd set the can on a fence post and it fell right over my head. A woman stopped in her car and jumped out—not to help, just to gawk. She shouted, 'What's wrong, what's wrong?' It was like she was ready to snap some pictures of me. There's too much of people just providing a spectacle for each other with nothing else to do down here."

"What do you think your father's attitude toward blacks and Indians is?" I asked.

"You'd know more about that than I do, I reckon, what with your talking to him so much. When I was growing up, Daddy and Mama was real particular about racial terms. If one of us said 'nigger' we'd be switched, and if a friend of ours said it it would be almost as bad. You can see what Daddy's done for Auntie Jess's family, and he did as much for the Bethanys before. These families sort of revolve around him and the farm work. Hell, Daddy's trained Jeeter, and that's all Jeeter has got. He don't give a damn about school and he'll probably never finish. Daddy's seen plenty of the rough living that goes on around these counties.

"The old man was pretty wild in his day, I believe. A fight would break out every time his band played. The bandleader would usually start it. Someone would make a crack about the song or the playing or the instruments and the leader would jump right off the stage and go to it. The second man, the piano player, would go next. The rest of 'em would keep playing as long as they could stand it.

"Daddy was sick as a child. He had to ride on the back of a buckboard wagon to go to church because the walk tired him. Once his appendix ruptured. He was walking home from school and fainted away and fell into a ditch. They found him after a while and carried him to the hospital. Whenever anybody wanted him they called around to all the houses and said, 'Find Archie boy.' He took violin lessons. He and Mama used to go dancing all the time. I guess he's had a pretty good life.

"I remember one time we had heard about a buffalo farm somewhere in the Piedmont, and Daddy and I went looking for it. This was in seventy-one or seventy-two. You know how Daddy travels—everybody's a friend, and we found that place just about by asking from house to house. It was near Pittsboro, but it turned out that all the buffalo had died. That's the way it goes. That's the way farms go, too."

/////

Later that night Waynette, Cathy, Alec, Julie, and Anne were playing Monopoly on the kitchen table. Archie and I had gone out to the porch. After checking on the tobacco in the morning, Archie had driven up to Clay Bank by himself and sat in the river. I could sense that something had changed inside him and I asked him what was up.

"Normally," he began, "the second week in July is when we harvest the tobacco. But this is the second week of August and it's time to start barning it. This is not so unusual for a dry year, and we did get that little bit of rain. Tobacco will sit there through a drought—that's why they say it's drought resistant. None of this is news to you, I know, but I went to the river today to try to figure out what has happened to the crop.

"When you put your sucker control on tobacco during a drought, it does something to it. It affects the quality, is what I mean. Tobacco will top out—put out its flowers at the top of the stalk—without moisture, but you will still have a stunted plant."

"So you topped the tobacco?" I asked.

"Yeah, we did that right before I took you down to the farm the first time. In fact, that was about the last work we've done all summer. It was about the end of June. What you do is you top the crop and at the same time you spray it with a chemical that cuts the growth of new stalk sprouts. Now all that's to throw the plant's energy into leaf production. So we topped at the normal time, but we used the sucker control when the plants were in a drought-stressed condition. I'd like to think that *that* is what I saw today when I looked at the tobacco leaves. I'd like to think that the problem is drought related, because if it's not, it must be a mistake I've made, which means it would be management related.

"You see, I got to thinking about when we sprayed for sucker control. There was this young boy helping me, and I handed him a quart container with a bit of some paint mixture in it. I told him to put it into the truck, meaning in the truck bed. Now he may have poured it into the spray tank that was in the truck. I didn't catch it at the time, and that paint mixture may have tainted the sucker control. As the spray tank filled up, this residue broke off from the bottom and floated up to the surface. Well, I have never put anything in that tank except for the sucker control. I figured that it was simply old residue of the same thing. But if it was paint, that would account for what I saw in the fields today.

"The residue was one-sixteenth to one-eighth of an inch thick. I wasn't thinking that it could be detrimental at the time. What I saw today was that the leaves have a twist in mid-rib. Now usually that's an indication of herbicide. Sometimes herbicide will drift in from a nearby field if it's windy enough when they're spraying. It could be the herbicide that they usually use on feed-grain crops. One time I had some tobacco that was messed up that way back in the sixties. I was farming the tobacco on share, and the tenant went off somewhere and thought he was buying cheap sucker control, but he had bought some herbicide cheap, and he ruined fourteen acres of tobacco that year. When they're working on share and don't know what they're doing they'll listen to whatever a neighbor says. If the neighbor says herbicide will do for sucker control, he'll go ahead and try it because it's cheaper. But what that stuff does to tobacco, it will make it grow out of this world. It grows itself to death. The cells simply explode.

"Since that rain the tobacco has started growing like that, and I can't account for it unless chemicals blew in from somewhere or that residue in the tank was the paint mixture, either or. Now, we've already received notice of a twenty-five cent reduction across the board, so it is going to be hard as hell to make anything at all on a crop that won't ripen."

Archie hunched over in his chair, placed his elbows on his knees, and slowly rubbed his hands together. "So, I've got this big-leafed crop that won't yellow, that's going to be of very poor quality—I can see that right now. And I'm going to spend a lot of time and money getting it out of the field, and I'll be lucky to make twenty cents per pound profit where normally I'm looking at seventy to eighty-five cents per pound profit. And corn and soy are a total loss. I'm looking at a deeper debt. And I'm looking at a ruined crop that, after all the goddamn drought we've had this year, actually had a chance down the home stretch. That rain could of made a damned fine crop out of it."

/////

For three nights and days the Clare family enjoyed being together at home. It seemed just long enough for the Clares' children to get restless. Waynette and her daughters went for walks, played games, went shopping. Anne, the youngest, still had many friends in Farlanboro and she spent a good deal of time visiting with them. Alec and Julie went to the river to swim and canoe. They asked me to go out into the back field with them to hit golf balls. Cathy read. Throughout it all the Clares planned for the beach trip. Every summer Waynette, Cathy, Alec, and Anne would rent a house at one of the North Carolina beaches—Ocean Isle, Holden Beach, or Sunset Beach. Archie usually went down for one night, Waynette for three or four, and the rest stayed the week with friends they had invited to spend a night or two.

Before they left, Cathy, Anne, and Alec had reviewed the things they were looking forward to or expecting at the beach. Anne loved the sojourn to Bird Island, a small uninhabited island that could be reached at low tide by wading across one of the river outlets from the Intercoastal Waterway. She claimed that one could find large conch shells off the point at the north end of the island. Alec talked of body surfing, of the luck it took to avoid the man-of-wars that littered the beach whenever a strong wind blew off the ocean and the skates that darted out from under nearly every step one took in the water. He had also brought a kite that he would fly, and horseshoes. Cathy spoke of her favorite bird, the black skimmer, which could be seen at sunrise and sunset skimming along a few yards offshore with its lower mandible scooping the water.

Even though Archie had decided not to go to the beach this year, he thought that he would wait another week before he'd start barning the tobacco, which meant that it would be mid-October before he'd finish. He started lining up his help, and it began to look as though the summer would finally come to an end. I would leave Farlanboro the next weekend.

/ / / / /

As soon as the family had left for the beach the house seemed extraordinarily quiet. Archie and I ate barbecue sandwiches and watermelon for lunch and dinner, and we went to the river in the afternoons. Archie turned off the air-conditioning in the house and left the doors and windows open all morning. He took several long naps. The first night Archie and I sat in the den off the kitchen. Archie had opened the door from that room to the outside, a door that the Clares never used.

The absence of the family, my impending departure, and Archie's awareness that in the next few weeks he would probably barn his last crop of tobacco seemed to put him in a mood for summing up.

"When I look back at my farming over the years I see that I started out the way I've ended up. During that job I had with the lumber company I had the time to do a little of what they call farming it on share. The tenants and the help come and go. The first tenant I worked with back then received half of the crop and paid rent. What I got out of it was hardly nothing. The tenant had cotton and tobacco.

He got to selling to another tenant and I'd be missing a sheet of tobacco every now and then. I finally told him he'd have to find something else to do. He left and I don't remember who took his place. I believe I had another tenant for a while. That Strickey boy, Fred Junior, I worked on shares with him for a long time. The Strickeys had what they call an International Harvester One-forty—good for tobacco work. It worked one row at a time. They had brothers who helped them barn it. I'd cure it. I had cotton then and I worked it. He worked the tobacco and I worked the cotton and we didn't have corn. I worked beans after cotton. Corn wasn't but eighty-eight cents a bushel. Got where nobody would plant it. I started getting on my feet after a couple years. The price of beans went up. Bought a six-fifteen combine and ran it three years and paid for it. Then in seventy-three I swapped it for a big combine. In the fall of seventy-two I had gotten my big John Deere tractor.

"I did a lot of custom work then. I'd go up in the rye-growing areas around Aberdeen, north in the Sandhills, where there was a large acreage of rye. They'd either sell rye for winter fodder or set cows loose on it. It does pretty good as green feed in winter. They didn't have combines up there. The price of corn went up during the Nixon administration and he revalued everything and everything doubled in price and beans really took off. That's when I got the combine paid for. I was in clear until the first drought in 1978. I believe then that's what broke me. That year I borrowed thirty-two thousand dollars. That's the debt I was fixing to finish paying for this year."

The ash from Archie's cigarette had grown long and he looked around for an ashtray. But before he spotted one, the ash fell into the cupped palm of his hand. He continued to hold the ash as he talked.

"I believe I did all right for the next three years until drought hit again in 1980. Took out another loan. I did all right, nothing to really make money. Now I had mortally made some money in 1973. When Nixon reevaluated, the bad news began—although we couldn't see it through all the profits. Your damn inputs—seed, fertilizer, pesticides—all that stuff started creeping up, and it got to the point where by eighty-four and eighty-five, along in there, hell, the chemical and machinery people were taking all the crop. Fertilizer went from fifty dollars to two hundred and fifty dollars for a ton. Many farmers are in debt now because they didn't take into account the difference between the cost of inputs and the market price for their product. It's just like the federal government. There will always be a tremendous federal debt. The only thing that I can say about the whole operation is that I'm glad I've held on to that old logging truck, since I'll need some way to dig myself out of debt."

I thought about what it would mean for Archie Clare to abandon his circuit. I couldn't imagine how he would spend his time. I visualized Archie continuing his daily drive south, swinging into the drive at Auntie Jess's, pulling up to the bulk barns at the Glencairn farm or up the long drive to George's just to observe, just to see what was going on. Of course, that was easy to imagine because that's about all I'd seen him do for the last two months. The degree to which this summer had differed from a normal summer was finally becoming clear to me.

"Because," Archie went on, "well, I know you've heard me say these things before, but you won't hear 'em again, brother, 'cause this is the old man's swan song. This is the end of farming for Archie Clare. And it's one year too late. If I could have gotten out last year, sold the equipment, rented the land, and leased the tobacco allotment, I would be in great shape right now.

"Of course, the way things go, next year they'll probably have a drought in the Midwest, and if they have one there and we can save the crop in the Southeast, then that might get all of the farmers out of debt down here. But that's the very reason I got to get out of the whole damn mess. It's getting to where you start counting on somebody else's failure to pin up your hopes. There's nothing in it. I'm working as hard as I can just to lose money. That's the long and short of what's going on right now."

"So is it the drought that's convincing you to stop farming?"

"The bottom line is that it's *everything* that's telling me to stop. Take the economy. When Reagan came in he started wasting all the money in the world on defense. Billions of dollars. So Congress had to do some cutting and boy, they jumped on lots of things. One of the things they jumped on was tobacco farmers. The government asked the farmers to pay back on their loans. They gave the flue-cured crowd five years to get rid of seven million pounds that had been stockpiled. If the farmers could get their business established again on a regular basis after that, it would be a good business with a profit in it. The tobacco farmer wouldn't have to be paying to support the price and to keep the surplus off the market. So on top of the problems due to drought, tainting of the crop, growing debt, and so on, I have the government's new policy flooding the market and undercutting my prices. Of course, I haven't said anything about the decline in demand for tobacco, but decline is a fact of the changing world."

"Does it bother you that tobacco causes cancer? If demand for tobacco is declining, isn't that a good thing?" I asked, cautiously.

"Well, *my* tobacco goes for chew as well as for cigarettes. But that doesn't make much difference—it doesn't get me off the hook is what I mean. Oh sure, it's as easy to justify growing tobacco as it is to condemn it if that's what you set out to do. It doesn't interest me much. We're a people who love to destroy ourselves. The things that we love literally tear us apart—eating, drinking, working, playing. Of course I've smoked for as long as I can remember. Whiskey and tobacco—they're choices people make. Drinking will kill you faster than smoking will. Fast cars, too. If you want something to worry about, look at all the farmers that get cancer from handling the chemicals they have to use to grow your wheat and your corn. Look at what you're eating every day.

"Used to be you could make a good living at tobacco. But all that's changed. Every year now seems we have a reduction in price because you got to pay to sell your crop—so much per pound. I figure that with the poor quality of my tobacco I might make twenty cents profit per pound this year, in 1986, when I could get thirty cents per pound in rent. And, hell, who wouldn't sooner rent it under circumstances like these? And that's what I'll do from now on. I'll take the rent, boy, and I won't have a regret in the world."

/ / / / /

Archie turned on the TV and found a channel that showed the Atlanta Braves playing the San Francisco Giants. He left the sound off and sat back down.

"The damn problem with farming—and everyone knows it—is not that there's too much land or that the weather is unpredictable. The biggest thing is the expense of raising a crop. You can easily spend a hundred dollars putting in an acre of corn. Used to could run the whole operation, all the crops I ran—corn, wheat, beans, tobacco—on six thousand dollars. That would pay for everything. The year before the drought I figure I borrowed nineteen thousand dollars. At the end of the year I owed thirteen thousand five hundred. That's where I made my mistake. The bank told me I had enough security for a twenty-two-thousand-dollar loan this year, 1986. So I borrowed the limit. Now I have two debts, the debt on this year and last and the debt on the drought of 1978. Now I have my loans arranged in two accounts, and they are down to nine thousand dollars and five thousand dollars or so. And you know something else—out of all this paying back, I paid back twenty-five thousand dollars in two years—all that money's been paid on debt, interest and principle. To top it off, the Internal Revenue Service said I owed nine hundred dollars income tax besides paying back the money on the loan.

"It's the government I'm talking about. It all goes back to the government. It all goes to damn bureaucrats and to those four tanks you saw on the highway today on the way to the river and to all those GIs you saw sitting around on the hillside next to the interstate. My point is that the government is draining us. It's taking the blood out of the people. The farmer keeps the economy going by having land he can call his own, but I don't know a farmer who hasn't got something mortgaged. You can't move without credit.

"It doesn't make sense. I'll tell you this—the farmers that are left in farming are there because they're stuck. They can't get out. And the banks, hell, they can't live without farmers' money. It's just tit for tat is what it is, a tit for tat deal."

Archie was throwing together all the complaints, all the bitterness that had grown within him during a summer of inactivity. There were a lot of people, forces, institutions, and policies that merited his anger. But I sensed that regardless of what he said about the banks, the government, or the chemical companies he really believed that the folly of farming was somehow an intrinsic part of the art of farming.

"Subsidies. Subsidies are just another form of security for the bankers, anyway. Farmers don't get anything for them. The banks need to write off some of these debts so that the security will be there. Imagine what will happen when all the old machinery goes. The farmers will have nothing."

Archie stood up and went into the kitchen. I paid attention to the baseball game for a moment and noticed that the players were wearing long-sleeved undershirts or turtlenecks.

Archie returned and watched a man on first base steal second. "That's just like the son of a bitch to run," he commented. I wasn't sure what he meant, and I asked him.

"You can see it in his eyes—he's trying to get something for nothing. Here you have all these blacks making millions of dollars playing a game. The thing that pisses me off is people who will do anything for money. When money becomes the end-all and be-all, well that's the ultimate corruption. It's not that blacks are unlike all the others. Just like the Jews. Just like the Germans. Hell, the French are the same and the Mexicans. And the worst of them all is the damn Scots."

What had appeared as the first overt indication of racism that I had seen in Archie dissolved, or at least was clouded by the extension of his contempt to so many groups.

"Farming will come back someday, but I'm too old to wait for it. You aren't guaranteed a damn penny until you already put in your time and money. It's a ten-hour-a-day job. If you're a mechanic that helps, but if not your work costs thirty-five dollars a damn hour—who can pay that?

"It don't make sense why I stayed in it as long as I did. I would come home, take a couple drinks, and go to sleep. I was working so hard I didn't have time to think about it all. I just didn't think. But now I've had time to think and I've drawn my conclusions. It ain't there. You lose every damn bit of your effort. It's a young man's job. Like George and his brother. George makes good money. He works four days a week sheetrocking. He doesn't drink, he's under forty, he's young. That's the kind of man it takes to farm. He's smart, too. He's young and he's smart. And he has a job to support him. He looks for ways to spend money to avoid paying taxes. Well, of course he farms because he likes it, but he also gets a tax shelter out of it. I believe that if they get the good seasons they need they'll buy all my old machinery. But they sure as hell won't buy that old combine. They'll buy a brand-new John Deere."

Archie stood up and walked to the screen door and peered out into the night. Moths and other bugs beat their wings against the door with a plop. Archie flicked the screen with his finger to dislodge it.

"The only regrets I have to the whole thing—I won't miss farming because I have come to dread the work—but I got to get a handle on this idleness. Living so far away from the land I farmed was a mistake. The idleness worries Waynette more than me. A lot of it's habit. If a person works twenty-eight or thirty years, then quits, it takes a while to get used to that. I think what it boils down to is in the winter cut firewood, maybe log a bit, pick up some kind of work in the spring and summer, have a great big garden and sell what you don't use, and find some hobby work to give you something to do.

"That's all a one-man farm is anymore—hobby work for someone who has another job. I don't have the money to travel, but that would be the most enjoyable thing. If I went to work the minimum wage is all I'd get. I won't get any training. They don't want to train you. Hell, your check is cut by a computer. There may be jobs that would pay well, but where are they and how do you find out about them? Back in sixty-eight, when I had difficulties, I was young and still had that drive. Back then it took activity, and then you had people available for sharecropping. Now all the young folks with energy are off working twelve-hour shifts in the canneries and textile mills. The inputs were all cheaper back then, too. And the machinery was new—you didn't have to fix it all the time. Oh, I learned a lot and I did a lot, but I still lost money. I ought to have more than debt to show for thirty years of labor."

Three thousand miles away, in Candlestick Park on the western edge of the continent, the cold ocean air stiffened the fingers of the outfielders and turned the pitcher's breath to visible vapor. The ballpark's lights were on, but light from the sky still shone blue against the arcing fly balls. One hundred miles southeast on the shore of the Atlantic, the Clares would be watching Orion wheeling above the lines of surf that glowed white in the darkness. Someone would drag a stick in the wet sand and see the phosphorus sparkle.

Archie turned off the TV and said, "Don't pay any attention to me. I'm the one that slipped up this summer. One way or another I let something ruin that tobacco crop, and that's what eats me. If I can't do any better than that, then I have no alternative but to quit."

//////

TEN

ARCHIE SET DOWN Bruce Catton's *Civil War* and let me know that Bruce Catton was a Yankee. The warm air of an August evening blew lazily through the screen door as Archie and I sat in the back room of his house.

"'Bout this time of night when we were young we'd go to the river and swim with the car lights on. We'd jump in and cool off and then head for home to sleep. And we would sleep well after that. That was *our* air-conditioning. It wasn't that hot back then—maybe ninety-five degrees would be the high. Never would see hundred-degree weather. We haven't been getting much rain since then. But this year looks like things are back to normal in our county, what with thunderstorms nearly every afternoon."

It had been an average August day: the heat had erased the early morning hours when we'd driven down to look at the leased tobacco and pick up some tomatoes. It was 1988, two years after the drought, and two years after Archie had quit farming. We had returned home for lunch and a nap and had driven out to the river on the long side of the day's heat. A storm cloud gave us twenty minutes of gray when we got to the river at Clay Bank. The wind rippled the surface of the river-bend pool upstream and leaves flickered green and white as they somersaulted through the air. Then we drove home. Then we ate supper.

According to the weather record, the autumn after the drought of 1986 had been like any other. Once the summer had finally turned the corner and begun to decline, the heat and drought that had shriveled hearts and sucked crops dry settled into the fine sediment of memory. But it seemed that the foliage burned more brightly and furiously and faded more rapidly that year than most others. And the nights were blacker, the air fresher, and the stars more distant. The rain that fell fell harder. And the rain that fell was augmented by another rain unlike any Farlanboro had felt for many years. Farlanboro had its share of storms and wet weather to break the back of drought, but it was the acorns that fell in bushels, that swarmed like locusts on the streets and fields, that said for certain that something had ended. And since the ending of one time is always the beginning of another, the hard rain of acorns inaugurated the renewal of the seasons' motion.

By the next spring the acorns had taken root amid the leaves and dirt in gutters and yards and raised their green fingers three inches toward the sky. In seven years, when the oaks that had suffered insurmountable strain during drought finally will yield to the seven-year-old dearth, the acorns will have unraveled their codes of green and leaf shoulder high, a fathom into fields of blue.

/ / / / /

News came during the winter of 1987 that Archie had followed through on his resolution to stop farming. He'd quit. That's the way he put it. Archie sent me a letter outlining his activities and enclosed a murky photograph of a snake in the bow of a canoe. He said he'd had enough of farming and that he'd gone to work in the woods as a one-man logging operation. Still, when I visited him that August of 1988 I shouldn't have been surprised to hear him talk about what he'd planted since he'd quit farming. After all, I'd been taught that the farmer preferred drought to too much rain, that he described as ideal an environment that alternately scorched and soaked his crops, that the dead were as alive to his mind as the living, that even when he was in debt the bank considered him an excellent candidate for a loan. It should have come as no surprise then that a farmer who had quit farming continued to operate his combine, persisted in checking his crops every day, and received government papers and bank loan statements associated with the business of sowing and reaping.

Earlier that spring Archie had put $350 into twelve acres of corn as part of a deal with George that amounted to another version of sharecropping. Archie disked the land twice to prepare it for the corn and told George to put on the fertilizer until he ran out. Fertilizer prices had risen 200 percent, Archie said, so farmers weren't putting on as much as they used to. They had come to realize they could get away with less.

"Out of the entire project I'll get a dollar-fifty at fifty bushels an acre, so eight hundred dollars," Archie said. "So my profit is four hundred and fifty dollars. Three years ago, in 1985, I got fifteen hundred dollars—at three dollars and five cents a bushel. Is it that there's a surplus of the product nationwide? No. The government and business are just doing what they can to pay farmers as little as possible for their crops. Are you, when you go to the supermarket, paying *half* of what you paid three years ago for your corn? Hell no. What's going on? Damned if I know. Boggles my mind. That's why I quit. It's a roundabout way to make four hundred and fifty dollars."

As Archie spoke he laughed and shook his head. He pronounced the last words with a singsong rhythm because he knew that he'd said the same things many times before. The bitterness had washed out of his words, if not out of his memory.

"It reminds me of the time the old farmer at the John Deere place heard the young farmer complain that he had thrown a rod in his cotton picker and it was going to cost him a thousand bucks. The old farmer said, 'Hell, I threw a rod in my cotton picker once, and all it cost me was a Moon Pie and a Coca-Cola.'" Archie laughed. Ever since he heard me curse when the snake fell into the canoe, Archie had been confident that it was all right to tell me dirty jokes. Now he could laugh about changes in his work that only two years before had broken his heart.

And that was a remarkable thing. In August of 1986, shortly after I had left Farlanboro to go back to school, Archie Clare had cleared only nineteen cents per pound at the market on his tobacco. The buyers saw, as Archie had seen, that there was something wrong with it. They did not label it dioxin tainted as they often did tobacco of inferior quality that bore evidence of chemical impurity, but it was the first year in a long time that Archie had sold his tobacco to the tobacco cooperative for the lowest price going.

A few weeks after Archie finished harvesting tobacco he did an extraordinary thing. He bought a ticket for a flight from Raleigh-Durham Airport to Buenos Aires and he flew to Argentina to spend ten days. He had intended to scout out opportunities for working as a buyer for the American tobacco companies, which seemed to be buying more and more tobacco abroad each year. He wanted to see if he liked the place well enough to live there, well enough to pursue a company position. He had been thinking that Argentina was the up-and-coming place, the next United States in terms of agricultural production. When he arrived in Buenos Aires after having changed planes in Florida, it was to ten straight days of rain during the Southern Hemisphere's spring. Archie had a connection there—the father of an exchange student who had gone to school with Cathy. Archie's new friend, however, proved to be very protective and kept a watchful eye on him. The political atmosphere in the wake of the Falklands war and the subsequent changes in the government may have been to blame. Archie got the impression that all of his Argentinean acquaintances were wary of him. Archie had wanted to visit the agricultural communities on the pampas, but it seemed to him that his host frustrated his every attempt to set off on his own and see the country.

Archie spoke a dozen words of Spanish at the most. He returned to Farlanboro with an almost overwhelming sense of the palpable mysteries of the world. As it will do for anyone, spending ten days amid strangers who speak a foreign language filled Archie with the sense that excruciatingly meaningful things were in the air if he only had the language with which to grasp them. The trip deepened Archie's appreciation for the familiar mysteries of corn and wheat and weather that he encountered at home.

/ / / / /

As things turned out, Archie was grateful he had hung on to the old logging truck. In order to pay off the farm debt, he fixed up the truck (which had sat idle for most of the last thirty years) and took it into the woods. The option of logging the timber on the land adjacent to the fields by Auntie Jess and Dan L.'s house had always been a card up Archie's sleeve. Just before leaving for South America in the fall of 1986, Archie had a logging company survey the tract. They offered him $16,000 for the timber. Archie was certain that he could earn three or four times that logging it himself, so that's what he planned to do. He logged during the winter, spring, and early summer of 1987.

In the summer of 1987, months after it had become too hot to spend much time logging, he took a job at the tobacco warehouse in Fairmont. Maybe he saw it as another avenue that might lead to a job as a buyer for one of the big tobacco companies. Even after his visit to Buenos Aires, nothing would have suited him better than to be sent to South America for a few months every year. But at the warehouse the tobacco dust tore up his lungs, and he sat out a couple of weeks at home in bed with a bronchial infection. The market work might have provided the perfect interlude in Archie's logging routine. It would have kept him in touch with the culture he knew best and leavened his isolation in the woods with the company of farmers and buyers. The other market hands, however, made a pastime out of playing cards. Archie didn't much care for cards, and once the tobacco dust took hold of his lungs, he didn't feel much like talking or listening or doing anything at all, really. By September, Archie was looking into a new line of work. He hoped to pick up a temporary job with the census people, who were surveying addresses out in the country. He thought he would like that work pretty well.

So Archie's life stayed the same in many respects. He continued to drive the circuit. He continued as his own boss. He often worked harder in the woods than he had as a farmer, but he still set his own pace and if he wanted to he could take a few days off after hauling a load of trees to the mill. He was still dependent on the weather, though, for if it rained too much he couldn't move the heavy equipment in the woods and swamp.

Archie had tried to break the circuit's hold, first by taking his trip to Argentina, then by working at the tobacco market and surveying for the census. But these forays out into the larger world remained brief excursions. The blank spot on the map that Archie knew as home worked on him like gravity; the rhythms of his heart had come to beat to the tune of the thousand nameless places within his daily rounds. Maybe it was that he wanted to watch the fields he'd farmed continue to yield to the farmer's hands. Maybe it was that he wanted to witness some variation of his own drama unfold with George at center stage. Maybe it was that he did not need a map in Lothian and Campbell counties even when he discovered a road he'd never driven down.

Waynette was just a few years away from retiring herself. Her high school had been responding to the education reform that had begun to sweep the country. She had been required to attend workshops after school. "After thirty years of teaching they're telling me I need to learn how to make lesson plans," she said in wonder. She began looking forward to getting out of the school system. As long as Archie had something to do, something to keep him from brooding around the house all day, she was content with the change in his occupation.

Auntie Jess and Dan L. had found some way to pick up work to replace the seasonal work they had done for Archie. And, until Archie could sell all of the equipment, they would continue to watch it for him. Archie and Waynette still took them baskets of butter beans to shell. Jeeter would graduate from high school in another year, but he had gotten into trouble with the law—joyriding in a stolen car with friends. He had taken up with kids from cities in the North whose dismayed families, trying to insulate them from drugs and crime, had sent them south to live with relatives. Cooter Tom had given up twirling in the dust as he began to shoulder the woes of adolescence.

/ / / / /

So, even as things changed, things stayed the same in the life of Archie Clare. The fields had turned green with the first blushing of spring, almost as if overnight. He knew that the transformation of the fields had come with the grinding of gears, the working of fingers, and plenty of sweat and worry, but some other farmer had undertaken those joys. Archie's tenure on the fields was loosening and he had begun to ask himself what differences the changes had brought. He still saw the crops grow and still reviewed in his mind the steps in the processes of cultivation and harvesting. He continued to toil in the gears of machines. He had begun his new life in the same old place with the same road ahead of him and behind him. He had not, however, taken out any new loans, and that was something. He had begun to pay off the debt without contributing to it, and that was something, too.

The less Archie had to do with farming, the more he became aware of just how much he loved its particulars. The names and stories caught at a produce stand as he thumped cantaloupes, the thrumming of the combine's engine as he turned to a new row, the stalks of Silver Queen green and luminescent around him as he broke the corn, the lightness in the palm of his hand as he held the seed for an entire crop of tobacco. He loved the details of raising, handling, cutting, and selling his crops. He loved the opportunities for sensation, for life in all of the particulars of his days. He came to appreciate even the paperwork required for the leasing of his crop allotments, even the smell of government ink and the feel of wrinkles on government paper.

"I reckon I'm going to get me a big balloon to take some of those trees out of the woods," Archie observed.

"How would you pick up trees from a balloon and keep the balloon away from the treetops?" I asked.

Archie smiled. "I reckon what I need is to buy me a helicopter." He laughed. "You believe that one, too?"

That morning in August of 1988 Archie and I planned to drive the familiar highway toward the Sinclair farm and the woods on Bootheel Swamp. He pushed his straw hat back off of his forehead, jabbed the gearshift, and pulled out of the driveway.

/////

As we drove south through Lothian County, the air teeming with bugs, the windshield coated with a film of crushed insects and insect wings, I saw the extent to which things *had* stayed the same. Intolerable heat, cigarette smoke, the El Camino's throbbing engine—these belonged to Archie's experience the way the dog-chewed upholstery belonged to the truck. Barney, slightly huskier than he had been two years before, swayed from side to side in the truck bed as he caught the wind in his open mouth. Pecan groves, pines, produce stands, tobacco barns, and cars headed north all slid by in a steady blur of clear images.

By making trees his business Archie had moved toward the large end of the agricultural scale. He became a reaper cutting forty and sixty years of growth in a moment. And the proportions of his new work seemed just about right, for he was dealing with a growth cycle that had the measure of his own life. Logging was hard work, but he found recompense in the solitude and the solace of the surrounding trees. And logging provided him with a sense of retreat from the indifferent machinery of paper farming and with a sense of return to the work of earlier days in North Carolina.

For months after the drought of 1986 the ground in and around Bootheel Swamp remained dry, and the lack of moisture made cutting and hauling trees comparatively easy. The wood became a way to ease out of farming. Until one crisp February day in 1988 when Archie had loaded a bunch of logs onto his truck and driven them to the lumber mill. As he was getting ready to unload, a log rolled off the truck, caught his back, and bent a vertebra.

/////

"First, in the fall and winter of 1986 and 1987, we went through and cut the big tulip poplar. That went for veneer, plywood. And then the next winter, 1987 and 1988, fall and winter, we went through and got the pine. Delivered that to the sawmill and started on white gum. Never did get into the cypress. There ought to be thirty thousand foot of cypress in there, maybe twenty-five to thirty big trees, but it's scattered all over the swamp and would be very difficult to get to. We cut maple. No oak. Have some big oak in there too, back on the river."

By June Archie's back had improved to the point where he could drive to the farms and the woods again. The mornings that spring had been cool, and many days it had rained. Archie had spent a lot of time on his back watching the weather return to the patterns he had known in his youth. By May the gnats were bad. There had been days when Archie had wondered if he would ever be able to resume logging. There had been entire weeks when he wondered if he would ever again ride in a car without a great deal of pain.

We were driving to the woods in Bootheel Swamp so Archie could show me the logging operation. As we drove he reviewed the details.

"Tulip poplar have to be eleven inches in diameter at the small end, the top. Pine has to be eight inches on the little end, white gum and maple ten inches. The biggest poplar was about three thousand board feet. Most of it ran in footage from about, oh, I reckon about three hundred foot. Now with pine, you cut a smaller tree with pine. With white gum it'd be eight hundred, a thousand board feet for five trees. What does that amount to? Well, white gum runs two hundred dollars per thousand board feet log scale, pine two hundred and eight dollars per thousand, and poplar two hundred dollars. The mills here don't want cypress. You have to sell it all at once to someone who is using it right then. If I were building a home I'd build it with cypress."

According to Waynette, Archie had begun talking about building a house down in the swamp. Cypress would have been the ideal wood for such a house.

"I've never heard of oak being used in weatherboarding. And oak is hard to get a nail into. Builders like fir, even here in the South. They can slap a nail into it, Bam!, with a machine. It's not strong like yellow pine, which has the layer of turpentine to give it strength. The sawmills here in town have all gone out of business anyway. There's no need here for dress lumber, and all they cut is pine. The lumber market must be mighty competitive. You'd think there would always be a demand for lumber, but around here there's not. And of course we utilized all the straight treetops for pulp. But they're so damn picky about it, the mills are. I have two mills I can haul to. One is just outside Wayfare, and the other is down by Fairmont, where the tobacco market is located. I took several loads up to one of the mills and they turned 'em down because they weren't straight."

We entered the dense forests along Bootheel Creek, which we crossed a few miles north of the Clare land. On the side of the road a crow that had been pecking at a dead opossum hopped out of our way as we passed.

"I was offered sixteen thousand dollars for the whole tract, and that was every tree in there. And we've already got more than that out of it and left a lot of trees. I invested about eighty-five hundred dollars for logging equipment, most of it—seven thousand dollars—in a bombardier. That's the machine that operates on a track the same way a tank does. It was designed for snow, but it works well in the swamp, and I use it to haul out trees that are too far back for the skidder to reach. The skidder—that's basically a truck with a cranelike arm mounted on the back and a spool of thick steel cable that's used to drag trees along the ground—well, it was left over from the sixties. I bought it back then when I logged plantation pine out at the McPhee property in north Lothian. It was thirteen or fourteen years old when I bought it. An ice storm came in and broke up all the pine on the McPhee land. So I went in with the skidder and cleared it up in order to salvage what I could from the disaster. And that was the reason for buying the skidder. It had been sitting in a swamp over here at Cullenfield in Campbell County. The old man who owned it wanted to clean it up, and I paid fifteen hundred dollars for it and wanted it first just to load logs with and found out later that I had more than I thought. It has a forward spool and a rehaul spool. You can run a line out with the machine to pull the big cable out into the swamp. It's a cheap but slow way to get logs out. Skidders were popular during the war years. Mine is mounted on an old Chevrolet truck. They used to mount them at Shreveport, Louisiana. Some of these old farmers would take their trucks down there and have 'em put on. Louisiana is nothing but a swamp, and the skidder is made primarily for swamps. The one I have came from there."

Archie had not lost his flair for details. Nor had his knack for analysis diminished. The numbers were as plentiful as before, only instead of describing price per pound and pound per acre they described board feet. His narratives about procedures now applied to the cutting, retrieval, loading, and selling of trees.

"Economically, my decision to log the tract myself has paid off. Well, who knows what will happen next? But so far it looks good. The big lumber company would have left a tract that would have been worthless for sixty years. They would have clear-cut it. Like it is now, since I've been so se-lective, there will be plenty of good timber in twenty-five years. We didn't cut anything we couldn't get at least three or four blocks out of. A block is the length you'd cut the tree into. The mills would give you a list of sizes. You were cutting it to fit the lathe is what you were doing."

Archie shifted in his seat as he drove. I noticed that the speedometer didn't work and that the little red gear indicator hadn't been replaced.

"Now that swamp, no one will buy that. They don't like to go into swamps anymore because they can find other tracts without getting into the mess of mud and water. But if I ever get over this injury I'll probably go in on the other side of the river. There must be close to thirty thousand dollars in that. I may get back in there. I'd rather do that than let it rot. I think it would only take one winter to clean it out. I could get that lumber out in three months with two or three good men."

As we drove I remembered the heat of that summer of 1986. I had become convinced that summer could offer nothing to Archie other than ruin, but I saw that he had rendered the summer powerless over him by changing seasons and learning the vocabulary of autumn, winter, and spring in the woods.

"In order to make anything, or in order to make any business worthwhile to the owner, in terms of logging, farming, anything else, he should do it himself. That's the way to get the maximum profit. Well, I'd had some experience, and I figured that the seventy acres in the swamp would be big enough to sell to some large logging company. As it turns out, doing the logging myself, I managed to make enough money. I suppose that when it really comes down to it, I'm swapping my machinery for the debt. I didn't lose my house. Didn't lose the land. Forty thousand dollars off the debt in three years. Not bad. I'm not doing a damn thing right now, and it will be two or three more months before I can sit and ride for longer and begin to think about work.

I'll have to see about this census work. If the back can't take it, I'll quit. I can't even ride up to the Sandhills and bring back peaches, which is a handy way to earn a few dollars. Still, when fall comes around again I'll have something to do. I'll be in reasonable shape by then."

He calculated his retirement earnings, which, between Social Security and land and tobacco allotment rents, came up short of $10,000 a year.

"If I go to work, that's after I retire, I can't get more than sixty-five hundred dollars or I have to pay Social Security. You make over that and they figure you haven't retired. Now rents are investments, and they run about fifty-five hundred dollars. Subsidies are income and have to be reported as such. Have to pay tax on that. In 1990 there'll be a farm bill coming up—they want to get rid of subsidies worldwide.

"Now the successful young farmer in this region, he's the one who hasn't had drought yet even though it's been all around him. He lives right next to his farm and he takes care of it. Looks after it better than I could. The successful farmer can't be idle. I doubt he'd do anything but buy new equipment with most of his profit. As far as travel, education, having a good time, he won't mess with any of it. He won't drink. Or gamble. But he loves the land, and he takes care of it. He works it to where he can get the maximum yield. Every year he tries something new. This year he uses more herbicide than he used to. He might get to where he doesn't want to use it anymore if it looks to be unprofitable. He's young. His family all pulls together. His young girl can run a four-rig cultivator. If they get into a jam, she can do it."

I wondered if he was thinking about Alec, about how things might have gone differently if Alec had stayed in Lothian County to farm with him.

Archie then told me casually that someone had burned down one of the old tobacco barns at the Glencairn farm in Campbell County. George had seen the barn on fire when he drove past it, and he called Archie to let him know. Archie drove out to the farm and watched it burn, but there was nothing else he could do. He sat in the truck so that he could make sure the fire didn't spread, and eventually he fell asleep. When he woke up the charred remains still glowed red-hot. He was reminded of the days and nights years ago when he used to cure tobacco with fires. Each of the old stick barns had to have about a cord of wood to burn during the curing, wood that the tobacco farmer had to cut in the winter. They would cut in January and February so it would be cured out by the time tobacco came in. In order to maintain control over the heat, most of the wood was cut from rail-sized trees, something like three or four inches in diameter. Archie said that he never was much of an ax man, and not even as a kid had he spent much time cutting saplings for the tobacco. The sapling ends would be placed on the fire and the farmers and their families would stay up all night to keep pushing the ends of the trees up into the fire.

"You had to stay around your barn then," Archie said. "Build the fire the first day. About the third day you'd raise the heat and you'd have a good fire to dry the leaves. And then, on the fifth to sixth days, to dry the stems, you'd make it even hotter. That's when you'd stay up all night."

Tobacco, he said, was a big deal then. The harvesting and curing made for a grand occasion, hard work, and faces grim but satisfied in the flamelight. Tobacco wasn't then the emblem of disease; it was just a weed that gave the taste of life and money. Tobacco allowed you to chew a bit of the earth and a bit of the season when you dipped from your pouch, and cigarettes were fuses that burned with sweet smoke as your life found its own way out.

We pulled off the highway at the farm and Archie threaded the El Camino through the ruts in the dirt road that led back into the woods. I could see no evidence of Archie's logging: the woods' border against the field appeared unbroken.

"Now I had already taken the logs to the mill when the accident happened," Archie mused. "I unhooked the chain from the truck and took it off the logs. I knew I had two short logs on there that the standards wouldn't catch. I put my hand on the logs to test them and they seemed to be all right. I went to the other side and started looking at my lugs. One of the lugs had been squeaking when I drove over to the mill. Something rocked the truck—I think it was wind from a transfer truck on the highway—something shook the truck enough to send a log off. I was crouched down by the wheel and the log went over my head and then caught my hip. It pulled a vertebra loose and cracked one side of it, the right side. And I undoubtedly pulled something else loose. That's why this lower rib is giving me trouble. You've got a floating rib down there and it may have gotten knocked in. It's the next one up that's giving me the trouble. You're getting near the stomach and lungs there."

Archie searched his ribs and stomach through his shirt as he spoke.

"The doctor said something about my stomach. Hell, they don't describe nothing to you. First thing when they get you to the hospital is they want to know who your doctor is. I laid in that damn emergency room from ten-thirty or so until four-thirty. They rolled me over toward an open door and said, 'You can smoke here, not back there.' Bunch of shit. One of those doctors, they wouldn't let him practice anywhere else, he gets ready to give me a shot and

he says, 'Archie, this shot will get you from here to there.'
Hell, he's a dope addict himself. Some of the private doctors are all right."

The invective that Archie had once directed toward the
companies that profited from farmers' misfortunes was
now saved for the doctor and the hospital.

"The last time I was in the hospital I was dehydrated. All
doctors are money crazy. Even the hospitals are the same
way. They're just making money off you. And then they
wonder why medical costs are so damn high. Well that's
the reason—you can't afford not to have medical attention.
They're all the same way; it's all the same pattern. That
man that saw me, he never even stripped down my back to
look at it. They look at X rays, scanners, and all that, but
he hasn't even seen my bare back. Well, doctors do everything indirectly. They wanted to know the medical back-
ground of my whole family. I said, I'll tell you: they all died
of cancer or heart failure, and that sure as hell must be why
I've broken my back, Doc. That time I was in for dehydration, I just got up and walked away. The nurse said,
'You're not going anywhere,' and I said, 'Watch me.' I was
fine and they wanted to keep me in there so they could get
more money."

We got out of the truck and walked down one of the logging decks that Archie had abandoned. What Archie called
the deck was the cleared area a few yards from where he
parked the skidder. He would drag a bunch of logs to the
deck with the skidder and from there would use the skidder
to load the logs onto his logging truck. Beyond the deck lay
the old logging road that had been cut into the swamp by
Waynette's grandfather from the highway to an old tramway embankment.

Even though the swamp lay behind the fields around
the house where Auntie Jess, Dan L., and Sudi Jane lived,

it seemed to occupy another world entirely. Waynette's grandfather had logged there back in the days of portable lumber mills, when a lumberman could pack up his saws and dismantle their housings like circus tents. From the clearing where we stood we could see the road taper off into the swamp and end at the creek. To the south and west the land fell away from the large stand of pines to the now saturated floodplain of Bootheel Creek. The remains of an old tramway bridge marked the only spot in the surrounding swamp where the creek bed could be defined. There the creek was a twelve-foot span of black water. In Waynette's grandfather's day, a small flatcar tram had run along rails on the embankment. Archie believed that the tram road had been constructed before Waynette's grandfather acquired the land.

Archie led the way. He pointed to poplar and cypress, the big ones.

"Those will be the money-makers," he said. "I could have had the company come in here and cut it, but they would only have given me a fraction of what it's worth. And they would have taken all of it. I can at least be selective. Leave something for the animals."

Beaver, muskrat, bobcat, deer, snakes, turtles, frogs, and birds—there was plenty of wildlife in the swamp, Archie told me. He said that a bobcat screech could sound just like a woman's scream.

The woods seemed to make Archie aware of the vulnerability of people in the world. "Families just get tired of fooling with their people. For example, Mama didn't have proper care. We had her over here for a couple weeks but she got dissatisfied. She'd go to Durham for a week or two, go to Roanoke, get tired of them, want to come home. She just couldn't get a hold of herself after Daddy died."

Archie paused, put his hands on his hips, and stretched his shoulders back. He surveyed the swamp with a serious look. We heard a plop from one of the pools.

"I think what killed Mama was a heart attack. She had fallen at home in the old Clare house in Wayfare and lay on the floor all day long. My brother Billy was living with her at the time, but I don't know how often he was home. I believe he came home late that night and when he found her he called the ambulance. If I remember correctly, she stayed in the hospital all the next day and died the next night. Daddy had a heart attack and died reading a newspaper after supper. He was sixty-seven. Had his first heart attack when he was fifty-two. And he'd had a stroke. His right arm was partially paralyzed."

Changing the subject, he pointed to a stand of tall hardwood trees. "To get those I'll use the tram road for a deck. I might could use the skidder here and go out in the bombardier to cut the trees. Whether or not the trees get hung up in the muck, we'll just have to wait and see."

The woods were still but for the buzz of insects and the whoosh of tiny whirlpools that formed in the creek as it brushed the trestle pilings. The sound of water moving in the creek resembled the sound a piece of paper makes when it is held aloft and gently shaken. A woodpecker drummed on a tree high up in the forest canopy.

/ / / / /

After returning to the truck and driving around the fields and back to Auntie Jess and Dan L.'s house, we crossed the highway and drove onto the eastern portion of Archie's land.

We surveyed the two dozen sandy acres where Archie usually grew his produce and saw only a few rotten cantaloupes and broken watermelon rinds. When we walked toward the loblolly woods to check the bombardier, Archie

pointed out a cluster of walnut trees and told himself to remember where they were. They'd come in handy someday.
A scrap of wind blew through weeds grown waist high over
melons and cantaloupes. Wild onion at our feet, a black
walnut husk half devoured by worms, a dry oak leaf dotted
with flake galls. We paused at a sassafras thicket where
wind palmed the bigger trees' single-, double-, and triple-
lobed leaves. From the ground around the trees nearly
leafless shoots rose like spikes four feet and higher. Archie
gripped one with both hands and yanked it out of the
ground. Sudi Jane, he said, boiled the roots and called the
tea "happy juice."

We descended a ridge of sandy grass and onions into the
flood bed of a small branch that fed into the Bootheel a
mile or so south. Underneath an army-brown tarpaulin sat
the bombardier. The bombardier, as Archie had said, was a
machine designed to haul things on snow, its wheels working inside metal tracks. It looked like a tank without the
gun turret. Archie bought it from a man who had bought it
in Vermont who had the same idea as Archie: to use it for
logging in a swamp. Archie can pull trees through the
swamp with the bombardier, but last December, before the
accident, the transmission had been popping out of gear,
and he only used it when the skidder wouldn't do.

We drove to the far side of the woods that border the
swamp to find Archie's most recent logging operation. On
the deck sat the skidder and a stack of logs. The skidder
looked like an old Chevy pickup that one might find in a
junkyard, only it had a huge cranelike arm that extended
out of the truck bed. The skidder arm made the truck look
unbalanced, as if it would tip over backward if any more
weight was placed on it. Archie had chained the skidder's
front fender to a large tree. All the truck's windows were
broken, and the chrome hardware, door handles, and fend-

ers were missing. There was no floor inside the cab. Connected to the drive shaft was a huge spool that sat on the truck bed. It wound and unwound the hauling cable. Archie had rigged a stick through the window in the back of the cab so he could manipulate the accelerator and gear shift from outside the truck. That way he could watch the logs and stop the line to prevent the cable from snapping if a log snagged. That's his second biggest worry—who knows but a flying cable might cut a man right in two? His first worry is the logs themselves.

"Once I decide what trees I want, I clear a deck, situate the skidder, and cut all the saplings and impediments in a ten-foot-wide swath down to the trees I want to cut. The skidder's cable stretches about two hundred yards. Once I have cut the road, I mark the trees I want down, and my stumper, the man who cuts the big trees, will saw down the marked ones and remove their largest branches. I walk the cable as it unreels down to the tree, loop it around the tree trunk behind a branch nub, and then walk back up to the truck to haul it in."

/ / / / /

I looked at Archie as we climbed back into the truck. He had not aged perceptibly. His face couldn't have grown any more thoughtful than it already was. If he seemed more relaxed than he had been during the summer of the drought, that was understandable. As he reviewed many of the details of that summer of 1986, I discovered that much of what I thought I had come to understand from our earlier discussions was mistaken. I wasn't sure whether I had misconstrued his words or if Archie had revised his own narrative of events.

Archie maneuvered the gearshift as he felt for the right gear and the El Camino pushed on in the sandy soil. Behind us the logging decks and roads were swallowed within a wall of green. The truck shimmied through the soil like a canoe in water. We drove north toward Farlanboro, and when the road emerged from the swamp and woods near James Station we could see clouds gathering in the sky. For a moment a wave of cool air chilled my arm and I drew it inside. Eventually we pulled into the Clares' yard and got out of the truck. The weight of another summer seemed to lift as we heard the melancholy cry of a hawk overhead. A slant of light fell through the trees and foretold the coming of the sweet hours of evening.

That Archie would risk a disabling accident and work out in the woods all alone—and many days it came to just that—testified to his appetite for solitude. One of the great advantages of hiring his particular stumper was that he too seemed content to work alone, so Archie could follow after him into the woods and have the day to himself. There were new symptoms of Archie's peculiar and paradoxical relations with his fellow mortals, as Waynette had told me. Archie grumbled every Christmas about giving and receiving presents. He would push back his plate and rise from Thanksgiving dinner and retire to bed before the rest of the family had helped themselves to seconds. I had noted that his voice sounded remote over the phone and that he never offered any news. He would punch out the perfunctory questions and answers as if the conversation served only to keep him from sleep. He would stand up in the middle of a TV movie, at exactly the point where the plot took its most interesting turn, and go to bed.

Yet he never seemed to tire of the circuit he drove. Oh, he would complain about the cost, the time, the wear on the engine of the El Camino, but he never did what he did when he tired of other things, which was to simply stop doing them. And he couldn't seem to get enough of some of the people he encountered on his drive. Whenever George was home Archie would swing by and talk farm for as long as he could keep George from his work. He had more to say to strangers he'd meet swimming at the river than to his own brothers. He still seemed to have a great appetite for the life stories of people he didn't know, and he continued to recite them to me. Often he would review an entire life in a couple sentences.

There were few friends or family members who could generate the interest that mere acquaintances held for Archie. Maybe it was his disappointment that his son showed no interest in carrying on the business of the farm that led him to transform hope for the future into a passion for the inaccessible. People whom he could not possibly know well or for long preoccupied his thoughts: the woman behind the counter who sold him cigarettes and with whom he held two minutes of conversation, the farmer he'd talk with at the gas station as the two of them pumped gas. He lived with long-dead great-grandfathers and aunts, colonists, and obscure Scots who settled in Connecticut 250 years ago. He lived with the patriarchs of Wayfare, his father and the other men who every Saturday sat on a bench on Main Street and tossed nickels to kids so they could go buy ice-cream cones. He lived with Joe E. in a place where Joe E.'s head had never grown delirious with pain or drugs, someplace where Archie spent many hours over many days talking to Joe E. by his bedside as darkness gathered, someplace where of course Archie would have been when Joe died. He lived with all the people whose stories haunted him with the allure of the remote and the successful, with the community of shades that occupied the blankness on the map.

The woods, up until the accident, had become a place where Archie felt comfortable. He thought about clearing some trees down where the creek came close to some high, sandy ground and building a house there. The woods could become home in a way that the parcels of land he farmed never could. Those acres of furrows and weeds and pines could host his thoughts with their interpenetrations of growth and barrenness, and they could feed him for a time, provide a place for his money to hold up in storage, the way honey is loaded by bees into the wax comb network of the hive. But the woods contained shadows like those that throve in his thoughts. A tree has a history that is to a man's life what a sea fathom is to his grave. There he could escape the intricacies, the ingeniousness, and the friction of agriculture's paper epicycles, those little retrograde arcs that governed him so remorselessly and turned his means and material into the soil's sandy sleep. Residence in the woods would mean staking a claim on his projection into the daily round of his wanderings, making his workplace his home. And if he left enough trees and was careful about locating the house, the business of the highway would never reach his ears if he didn't want it to. He would enter into the conversation of the living and perform his excursions into the world of commerce with the deliberateness of will rather than the resignation of necessity. Whatever nuance of flight or shade of sunlight he sought hunting bird, whatever possibility skittered away into the next thicket, whatever star shone brightest in the constellation of beggar-lice on his coat shoulder, it would always be just outside his door.

But instead of moving to a life in the woods, Archie found an even more restricted world on the edge of Farlanboro. One February day in 1988, he had been arrested by a nick of time, by a tree he'd cut that had rolled over to cut him in turn. Now Archie Clare would have to wait and see if he could resume a life in the woods.

/ / / / /

That warm August night in 1988 I sat with Archie in the house on the edge of Farlanboro. As I thought about the day, a sweet scent like that from a second bloom of honeysuckle blew through the screens of the open doors. Underneath the whirring machinery of the night's insects and the business of the wind in the trees I could hear the rumble of a train in the distance and the intermittent sounds of traffic and the roar of the crowd at a softball game.

I imagined that someday something will change in the life of Archie Clare. It will be a time when people say he went the way of the southern farmer and he becomes just a name in the conversations about younger days. It will be a time when the economic measurements of his life evaporate and leave behind only the salty residue of words. It will be a time that has marked the end of a particular drought. It will be a time that looks forward to the next drought. It will be a time for the seed that he once was to begin growing in the fertile soil of the imagination, a time to fill in the blank space on the map with a name. It will be a time when he stops waiting for rain.

When the poet said that every person is the seed of a ghost, he had considered his mortal situation under circumstances similar to Archie's—the weight of time wringing water from his bones as he devoted himself to actions and productions that necessarily failed him, as he made a business out of scrawling on the fine-curved feather line between persistence and dissolution. But the seed, the man, the crop, the drive: these are the least of what they become. Farewell, farmer. Hello, son. They keep coming. They never, always fail.

I imagine it will begin as if we were driving down the familiar roads. We will pull down a long drive, dip and bounce and spot the tomatoes that he was after. Someone will have told Archie to come by and yet not be there himself, having driven to D.C. with a truckload of produce. Tomatoes will hang in a green air, tomatoes bruised by moisture, split by heat, engorged with their own water-soaked meat. Their large lobes will have grown like the chambers of an inert heart frozen in mid-pulse, will have grown into ribbed sections that bulge like fists of knuckles. An acre of tomatoes always was, always will be a messy thing.

Standing on the right-hand side at the end of the driveway will be a cinder-block house whose roof has turned to rust. Archie will shift uneasily in his seat before we roll to a halt. Driving will once again be difficult and the trip to the farm will be about all he can manage. The extra time to drive and pick up tomatoes, well, he won't be able to afford it every day. The house will rise up out of a thicket of sassafras and cane underneath live and willow oaks. Lightning rods, a whole crop of them, will grow from the roof like onion bulbs beneath alternately jagged and needle-straight spires. They will range in length from three inches to three feet and the sheer number of them will suggest that the house itself is wired to the sky. Whether designed to attract or dissuade the storm's river of electricity by shuttling the blazing lightfall to the easy earth, those wires will seem to have swollen a whole field with current.

We will poke around the yard, for it will seem that no one is home. Archie will knock on a window. A young man will answer him and he'll say, "Hey, old man, come on in and tell me the news!" And he will. Archie will open the door and disappear inside.